Breaking Into Salesforce

Salesforce

THE ULTIMATE GUIDE TO BUILDING
A HIGH-IMPACT CAREER

DEREK DAVIS

ISBN 979-8-9883640-4-7 paperback
ISBN 979-8-9883640-1-6 eBook
ISBN 979-8-9883640-2-3 audiobook

Interior Design by: Farhan Shahid
contactus@andromeda-productions.com

Table of Contents

FOREWORD

As a 10+ year Salesforce veteran, I can attest to the fact that the demand for Salesforce talent has only increased over time, making it an even more prosperous career path than when I started. And there's a multitude of options for not only those with an IT background, but also for those that lack technical experience.

The beginner's challenge with any journey worth taking is knowing where to start, and how to chart a successful path. Fortunately, "Breaking into Salesforce" is your ultimate resource for breaking into the Salesforce industry. It covers all the essential topics you need to know to become a successful Salesforce professional, including the necessary certifications and qualifications, how to create an attention-grabbing resume, and tips for using LinkedIn to attract targeted attention.

You'll find invaluable advice inside these pages on how to prepare for job interviews, negotiate salaries, and succeed in your own Salesforce career. Whether you're just starting your career in Salesforce, or you're an experienced professional looking to take your Salesforce career to the next level, this is the right book, at the right time, for you.

When I discovered Salesforce as a viable career option, I appreciated how accessible the platform was in enabling me to create enterprise level applications with clicks instead of code. I soon discovered that the Salesforce platform not only empowered me to create amazing apps, but also an amazing career. I am confident that you will find immense value in investing your time in learning Salesforce and leveraging the actionable insights provided by Derek Davis in "Breaking into Salesforce"!

Happy learning and I'll see YOU in the Cloud!

Mike Wheeler

INTRODUCTION

This book provides a comprehensive guide to advancing your career in Salesforce Administration. With the demand for Salesforce professionals on the rise, this career path is not only in-demand but also highly achievable. You will gain a deeper understanding of the benefits of a Salesforce.com career, as well as a detailed overview of everything you need to do to prepare for a Salesforce Administrator job, including tips for researching the job market, gaining insight into earning potential, and landing the right job.

You will also learn how to leverage your prior non-Salesforce experience to secure a related role in your industry, write an attention-grabbing resume, and use LinkedIn to attract job offers. Furthermore, you will be equipped with the tools to prepare for an interview, tell stories that effectively convey your skillset and value, and negotiate your salary and benefits package.

Additionally, you will gain an understanding of the Salesforce Administrator Certification Exam and software development lifecycle, as well as tips for requirements gathering to help you succeed in your job once you receive an offer. Lastly, an overview of different Salesforce roles will provide a better understanding of the Salesforce landscape and the various career paths you can pursue within the industry. This book has everything you need to know to advance your Salesforce career.

Climb to New Heights in Your Salesforce Career

SCAN ME

QR CODE Placement

This book is equipped with QR Codes for an enhanced reading experience.

Simply use the camera on your smartphone to scan these codes whenever you encounter the "SCAN ME" prompt throughout the pages.

Why Salesforce?

1.1. Why is Salesforce.com so Popular with Businesses?

Salesforce.com is one of the most popular CRM (Customer Relationship Management) systems on the market today. This is due to its intuitive design, user-friendly tools, and industry applications that allow businesses to better interact with their customers, partners, and employees. It provides users with an unparalleled level of business intelligence as well as real-time access to customer data; helping them make decisions that enhance relationships and drive sales. Salesforce also offers robust security measures, which makes it a reliable and secure platform for organizations to trust their sensitive data to. The scalability of the platform also makes it an attractive choice, as businesses can use it as they grow—allowing them to increase or decrease the number of services they rely on as needed. In short, Salesforce offers all the tools necessary for businesses of all sizes to access critical data quickly and easily while reducing costs at the same time—making it one of the most popular CRM systems currently available.

1.2. Why do Businesses Need Salesforce.com Administrators?

Businesses need Salesforce.com Administrators to ensure the smooth operation of their CRM system and its data. A Salesforce Administrator is responsible for the setup, maintenance, and support of the software, as well as customizing it to meet the needs of their organization. An Administrator will also be able to track user activity on the platform, identify areas for improvement, and keep up with new features as they become available. They can provide invaluable insight into a business's operations and make sure everything runs smoothly. By having a proficient Salesforce Administrator on hand, businesses can be sure their system is constantly running efficiently and that any issues are quickly resolved.

1.3. Benefits of Starting a Career in Salesforce.com Administration

Why consider a Salesforce.com related career? Over the last decade, tens-of-thousands of people have taken the plunge into starting a career in Salesforce.com Administration. With its ever-changing landscape, beginning a career as a Salesforce.com Administrator can be quite the challenge; however, you will find that this is overall an extremely approachable career option. It can be incredibly rewarding and offer plenty of growth opportunities. In this section, we'll cover some of the key reasons why you should consider starting your career in Salesforce.com Administration, as well as some insights into what you should expect as you get into your new career.

> **Here are some of the reasons thousands of people just like you have considered a Salesforce.com related role:**

1.3.1.   Grow From Entry-Level to Serious-Skills in a Relatively Short Time!

First and foremost, getting started as an administrator offers an incredible opportunity to learn new skills. You will be able to develop expertise in a variety of areas, including customer relationship management, software configuration and customization (no code required), data analysis, workflow automation, system security, user support, and more. These newly gained skills will be invaluable as you look to move ahead within your career or even start your own business down the line. Becoming an effective Salesforce Administrator could open up many doors since these specialized qualifications become even more sought after over time with further experience and additional certifications. Many find themselves moving up in the ranks faster than they thought possible. It doesn't take long to develop a serious skillset that allows you to add major value to businesses in any industry. As you add experience and credentials on your resume, you'll quickly be in the position to land higher-paying roles with even greater job security!

1.3.2.   Serious Salary Opportunity

The average salary for a Salesforce Administrator is approximately $88,000 USD per year. However, salaries can range from $60,000 -$130,000 USD depending on experience, location, and the size of the company. Like most careers, salaries tend to be higher in larger cities such as San Francisco and New York City, but thanks to the high demand for Salesforce.com Admins, and remote work potential, it's possible to live almost anywhere in the US and earn a six-figure salary by working in a Salesforce.com related role. You most likely will not start off in the top of the salary range, but as you gain experience and earn additional certifications, you'll find increased opportunities for higher earnings.

1.3.3.   Career Growth Potential

Salesforce is a highly sought-after skill in the job market, and demand for qualified Salesforce administrators is consistently high. Becoming a Salesforce administrator can open up new career opportunities and lead to promotions and higher salaries.

In addition, the role of Salesforce.com Administrator can serve a launch pad for many other related Salesforce job roles including:

- Salesforce.com Developer
- Salesforce.com Project Manager
- Salesforce Architect
- Salesforce Consultant
- Business Analyst
- Scrum Master

- Product Owner
- Marketer
- Operations Manager
- Sales Manager
- Service Manager
- and more...

1.3.4.   Remote/Work From Home Potential

Another major advantage is being able to work remotely, as there is now an increasing number of work-from-home Salesforce positions available. The flexibility that comes with remote working could make it easier for you to fit your job into your lifestyle, which could reduce stress levels all round.

1.3.5.   Versatility & Options

Salesforce is a platform that is used by a wide variety of industries, so a Salesforce administrator can work in a range of different career fields. Not only do you have the opportunity to work in an industry of interest to you, but you can also specialize as an admin on different sides of the Salesforce.com platform. Some people enjoy focusing on better enabling the Sales Team within an organization, while others may prefer a focus that is geared more toward Service Teams, and still there are others who enjoy working with both Sales & Service to provide a 365-degree view of their customer. A Salesforce.com career can be somewhat like one of those "choose your own adventure" books that you may remember from your childhood. Initially, you may just need to get whatever job you can within Salesforce in order to get some experience under your belt, but within a short 12 to 18 months you will find interesting options, and you'll be able to be more selective in choosing a job role that aligns closely to your personal interest.

1.3.6.   Positive Impact

As a Salesforce Administrator, you will be responsible for helping organizations to streamline their processes and improve their customer relationships. This can have a positive impact on the success of the organization and can be personally rewarding.

1.3.7.   Job Security

Salesforce is a leading customer relationship management (CRM) platform, and it is used by many organizations worldwide. This means that there is a high demand for qualified Salesforce administrators, which can provide job security.

1.3.8.   Benefits Recap

Becoming an effective Salesforce.com Administrator could open up lots of career opportunities in the long run since the skills become even more specialized over time with further study and experience. Having certifications like these on your resume can enable you to move up in the ranks faster than other people and land higher-paying jobs with an increased level of job security. So, if you're looking for stability and career satisfaction—both emotionally and financially—then starting out as a Salesforce Administrator may be just right for you!

1.4.   Roles and Responsibilities of a Salesforce.com Administrator

There are a number of things that could happen in a day-in-the-life-of a Salesforce Administrator. Basically speaking, a Salesforce Admin could do anything from setting up new users, helping existing users with password resets, modifying profiles to grant a user more or less visibility to records based on the needs of the business, creating reports/dashboards for business leaders and users to gain insights and make more informed decisions, and much more. Below, we outline some of the common things that can be expected of a Salesforce.com Administrator. Don't worry if you don't understand what all this means yet, just keep going down the path and you will soon get it!

COMMON THINGS A SALESFORCE ADMIN MAY DO:

01 Configuring and customizing the Salesforce platform to meet the needs of the organization, including creating custom objects (a table to store data in), fields, and workflows.

02 Managing user accounts and permissions, including setting up user profiles and role hierarchies.

03 Analyzing business processes and identifying areas where Salesforce can be used to streamline and improve efficiency.

04 Providing training and support to users on how to use Salesforce effectively.

05 Generating reports and dashboards to help stakeholders track and analyze key performance indicators (KPIs) for their business.

06 Troubleshooting and resolving technical issues that may arise with the platform.

07 Working with developers to create and maintain custom solutions within the Salesforce platform.

08 Keeping up to date with new features and updates to the Salesforce platform and implementing these newly available features as needed.

09 Maintaining data integrity and ensuring that data is accurate and up to date.

10 Managing integrations with other systems and applications (this often involves working with Salesforce Developers, who will typically do most of the heavy lifting for technical integrations).

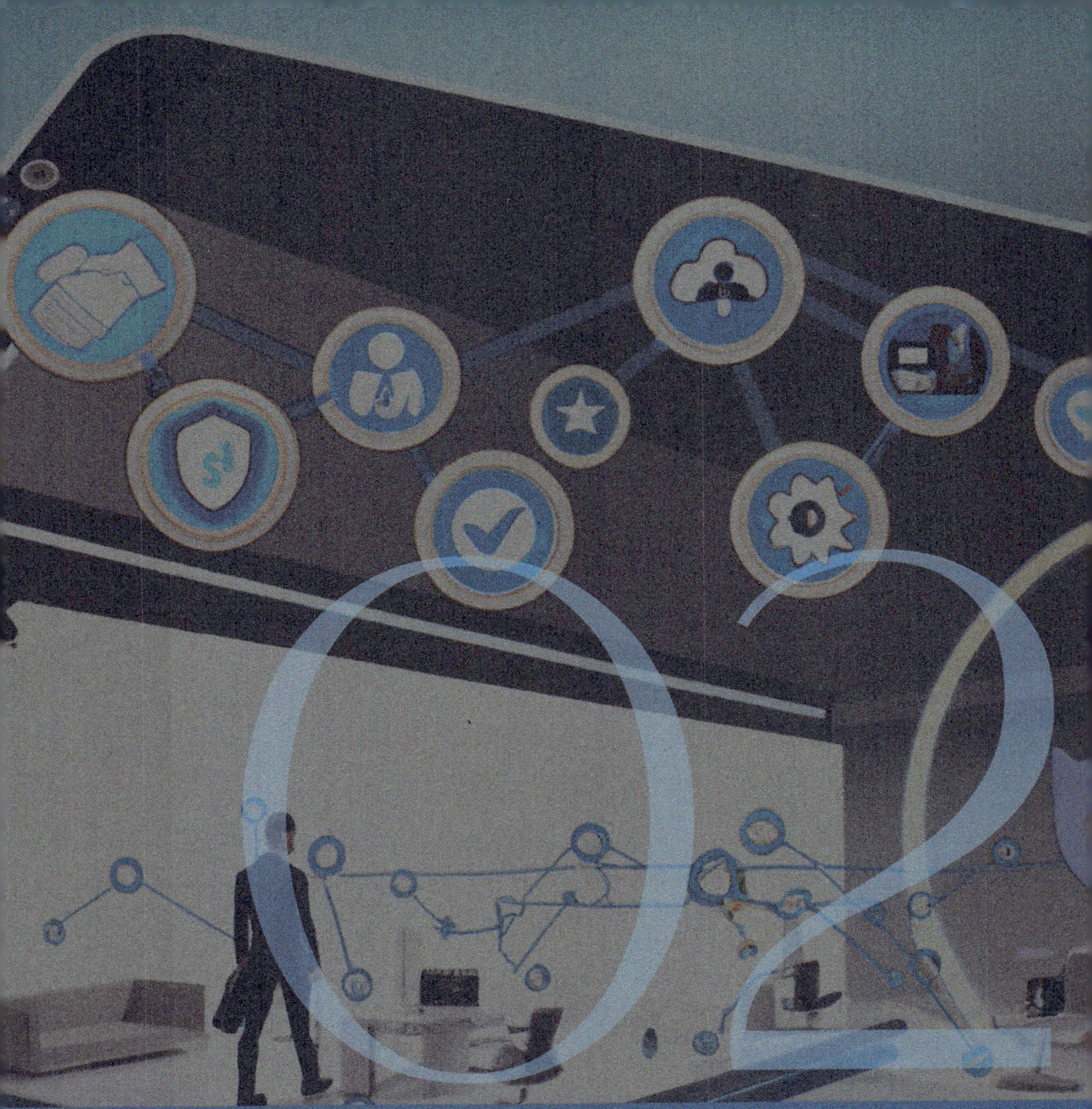

02

Preparing for A Salesforce Admin Job

2.1.   Certification + Experience = Job

Generally speaking, a certification + some experience = a job. The certification process is pretty straight forward (we will cover the certification process in greater depth in a later section). However, there is somewhat of a 'chicken and egg' type of scenario when considering how to get Salesforce.com Admin Experience when you don't have a job as a Salesforce.com Admin. This dilemma can be somewhat more challenging to overcome based on your background. We will cover this and other items in this section.

To successfully prepare for a role as a Salesforce.com Administrator, it is important to have knowledge of the Salesforce platform and its components. Most of these details will be learned as you go through the certification process, but here in this section we will go over many of the most common questions that are asked or should be considered when starting down the path of a Salesforce.com Administrator:

2.1.1.   Does being a Salesforce.com Admin require knowing how to code?

No code is required as a Salesforce.com Administrator. A basic level of familiarity with HTML, CSS, JavaScript, or Apex code can be beneficial if you are planning to later pursue a role as a Salesforce Developer, but it's certainly not required to be successful in a Salesforce Admin role. You'll have the opportunity to learn these things later in your career if you should choose to, but Salesforce is largely a "Declarative" platform. Declarative simply means that no code is required; most configurations can be done by 'pointing and clicking' through the various interfaces.

2.1.2.   What skill set do I need to be successful in this role?

The skill set required to be successful as a Salesforce Administrator includes having an aptitude for problem solving; familiarity with customer relationship management; the ability to communicate clearly with technical teams, clients, and stakeholders; and the ability to quickly learn new technologies. Much of this ability comes with practice. I have heard a number of Salesforce Admin success stories from stay-at-home moms or people such as school teachers, and many others, who come from a variety industries that are completely unrelated to technology. The technical concepts that are required can be learned!

To more specifically outline the technical skills needed to be successful as a Salesforce Admin, you'll need a general knowledge and understanding of concepts like: object oriented relationships, Salesforce automation methods, and validation rules; experience with integrations and data migration tools is a plus, but not initially required; a basic knowledge of system security and best practices will also be required to manage the Salesforce Org (Note: "Org" is common Salesforce lingo for "Environment").

Once you have enough knowledge, you can get a Salesforce.com Certification. Certifications are a good industry level standard to help employers understand the baseline of knowledge and skills that you possess. We will talk much more about Salesforce.com Certifications in a later section.

HERE ARE THE TOP 5 CHARACTERISTICS OF A SALESFORCE.COM ADMINISTRATOR:

Excellent problem-solving skills:
A salesforce administrator should have a strong understanding of the platform and an ability to find solutions to complex issues.

Technical aptitude:
Having the ability to figure out technical processes can be a great asset for Salesforce administrators, as they often need to perform various system configurations.

Good communication skills:
A Salesforce Administrator is required to interact with end users, they should have strong communication skills in order to understand the user's needs and explain technical concepts in plain language.

Detail-oriented:
Salesforce administrators must pay close attention to detail in order to ensure data is accurately entered into the system and integrations are properly set up.

Understanding of security protocols:
With access to large amounts of customer data, Salesforce administrators need to be aware of appropriate security protocols in order to protect businesses information from malicious actors and ensure compliance with Salesforce.com best practices.

2.1.3. How much experience do I need to have working with the Salesforce platform before getting a Salesforce Admin job?

There is no one answer to this question. The amount of experience you need will vary based on your background, related skillset, and the specific job that you are applying for. For example, you may lack Salesforce experience but come from a programming background that gives you enough related skills to make the employer feel comfortable that you will be able to catch on quickly. On the other hand, you may have zero computer programming experience but a lot of experience in a sales related background and you're familiar with the end user capabilities of Salesforce. This too can be extremely valuable if you make the transition over from being an end-user with a Salesforce Org to being the Administrator of an Org.

2.1.4. What type of certification should I pursue if I want to become a Salesforce Administrator?

There are a number of other Salesforce certifications available to pursue, and each certification focuses on different aspects of the Salesforce platform, but initially just stick to the basics. The certification that most employers will want to see is the Certified Salesforce Administrator certificate. You can always add more certifications after you land your first Salesforce job, and this will help you advance your career over time.

If you have some experience with Salesforce as an end user, then you may consider starting with the Salesforce Associate certification and then progress to Salesforce Certified Administrator. The Admin Certification is really all you need to pursue a career as a Salesforce Administrator, but you if you have a background as a Salesforce user, then you would still learn a lot in going through the process of obtaining your Salesforce Associate certification.

As an additional note for those who are coming from a related background (perhaps Microsoft Dynamics or other CRM); if you find that the Admin Certification comes easy to you, then you may also want to consider the Salesforce Certified Advanced Administrator certification, as having multiple certifications will make you a more appealing candidate when interviewing for Salesforce Admin jobs. Again, this is certainly not a requirement, but the more certifications you can obtain over time, the stronger candidate you will be.

2.1.5. Will I be able to perform all the administrative tasks on my own or will I need help from a team of developers?

As a Salesforce Administrator, you will be able to complete most administrative tasks on your own. Administrative tasks basically include any configuration within the Salesforce Org that does not involve code.

However, depending on the size and complexity of the Org, you may work with a larger Salesforce team and require assistance from additional team members for more complex configurations, such as automating processes with APEX code or integrating your Salesforce environment to other systems. These team members could include Salesforce Developers, Architects, or other technical personnel to build more complex integrations and automation. Typically, you will be working to support them as they perform these more complex tasks, but you as a Salesforce Administrator will not be expected to perform this level of tasks yourself.

2.1.6. What kind of support is available for Administrators and how can I access it?

As a Salesforce Administrator, you have access to a variety of support options. The primary go-to for a new Salesforce Admin will most likely be Trailhead and the Salesforce Support Community. You can find helpful tutorials and guides on Trailhead—Salesforce's official learning platform—and the Salesforce Support Community provides users with access to an online forum where they can connect, share insights, and collaborate with other professionals in the Salesforce platform. From technical advice to creative problem-solving, the community offers a wealth of resources for users to learn and grow their skills. With discussion boards and resources from Salesforce experts, this community is the place to go for all your Salesforce questions and needs. For example, you can contact the Salesforce Customer Support Team at any time by opening a case within the Support Community, or you may specifically outline a problem you're facing and ask a question within the user forums and receive answers/suggestions from different experienced Admins/Developers from all over the world. There are currently over 800k members of the official Salesforce Support Community.

In addition to the official support community, there are also various user communities available online within Facebook Groups and other platforms, such as the "SALESFORCE

Discussion Group" on Facebook with more than 35k members or the "Mike Wheeler Media Student Group," also on Facebook, with over 11k members. These are all places that allow Salesforce Admins and users to ask questions and get answers from experienced Salesforce administrators.

2.1.7. Are there any other specialized certifications that may make me more qualified for this role?

You should initially just focus on the basic Salesforce Administrator Certification... but yes, there are a number of specialized certifications that may make you more qualified for a role as a Salesforce Administrator. For example, the Salesforce Certified Platform Developer I certification demonstrates your knowledge in developing custom applications using the Lightning Platform. Additionally, the Salesforce Certified Community Cloud Consultant program can demonstrate your expertise in building and managing Salesforce Communities. You may also consider obtaining the Service Cloud Consultant or Data Architecture and Management Designer certifications if you plan to build and manage advanced customer service experiences or data integrations with external systems. These more advanced certifications will most likely be something that you consider over time. They are not required to get started!

2.1.8. What are the most common challenges faced by Salesforce Administrators and how can I best prepare myself for them?

Salesforce Administrators often face challenges such as staying up-to-date and familiar with the platform, managing user permissions and settings, and troubleshooting issues. It is important to stay current on Salesforce product updates and releases. Additionally, it is also helpful to practice troubleshooting scenarios in a sandbox environment before applying them on the actual system. Finally, it is important to set up comprehensive user permission sets that are tailored to each individual's needs while ensuring they are secure and compliant with best practices.

Facing Challenges?
Ask The Community

https://admin.salesforce.com/

SCAN ME

2.1.9. What are the technical concepts that I need to know when first starting as a Salesforce.com Administrator?

As a Salesforce Administrator, you will need to become familiar with the following technical concepts: object and field creation, validation rules, workflow rules, process builders, user roles & profiles, sharing settings and security controls. You should also have knowledge of out-of-the-box reporting capabilities so that you can quickly build reports with custom fields and filters.

A Word of Encouragement

This may all sound overwhelming at first, but please allow me to digress for one moment in order to offer you a little comfort... When you are studying for a Salesforce Certification Exam, you are expected to understand a moderate amount of information and concepts over a wide variety of content. This can make these exams extremely difficult at first. However, to contrast that, when you begin your career as a Salesforce.com Administrator you are typically only required to know what is needed for the situation at hand. In addition, you get to research it, read documentation, reach out to other Admins within the Success Community, test solutions in a sandbox, and do whatever necessary in order to find the answers that you need.

For example: your boss is never going to come to you and say, "Tell me a moderate amount of information about a wide variety of Salesforce.com concepts." No, they are going to come to you with a specific problem, and when they do, you'll have the opportunity to respond. At first your response may be with follow up questions to ensure that you understand exactly what problem you are trying to solve, which users are experiencing the problem, and when/where they experience it. Then you can simply say to your boss, "Let me look into that, but I'm sure we can overcome this." Then you get to work! You get the opportunity to replicate the specific issue in a sandbox and make the changes you believe are necessary. If you don't know what changes to make, then you can commence the Google searches, reach out to the Salesforce Success Community, or consult other resources on your team to get additional assistance.

So don't fret about how much you need to know at first to do the job! The reality is you need to know enough to pass the exam, and then you will figure your job out one day at a time. Within six months, you'll be confident in your skill set and no longer have "imposture syndrome".

2.1.10. How can I get Salesforce.com Admin experience if I don't have a Salesforce Admin job?

There are a variety of ways to gain Salesforce Admin experience even if you don't have a job as an Admin. You can take online courses and certification programs, complete hands-on Trailhead activities, or find volunteer opportunities with nonprofit organizations who use the platform.

CatchAFire.org is a great site to check out if you're looking to volunteer for a non-profit organization in exchange for Salesforce.com experience.

2.2. Researching the Job Market

There are many ways you can begin your own research to learn more about the Salesforce. com Admin Job Market. Here are a few suggestions of where to start:

Search online job boards:
Look for job openings on websites like Indeed, Glassdoor, and LinkedIn. You can also use specific job search terms like "Salesforce administrator" or "Salesforce admin" to find relevant job listings. Additionally, you can use Glassdoor to read reviews of companies hiring for the position, which may provide insight into salary, company culture, and other important factors.

Find & Join
Local Salesforce
Groups
http://TrailblazerCommunityGroups.com

Network with professionals in the field:
Connect with other Salesforce administrators or professionals in related fields to get a sense of the job market. You can join professional organizations or attend events and conferences to meet and talk with people in the industry. You can also follow industry blogs and join user groups on social media platforms such as Twitter and Facebook to stay up to date on the latest trends in the Salesforce administration field. Many different cities have local chapters of Salesforce user groups and admins.These can be a great opportunity to meet people in your local area and network. Be sure to check out *https://TrailBlazerCommunityGroups.com/* to join groups to meet and collaborate based on your location, role, and interest.

Research salary data:
Look up salary data for Salesforce administrators to get an idea of what you might expect to earn in this field. Websites like Glassdoor, Salary.com, and the Bureau of Labor Statistics can provide useful salary data.

Also consider some industry specific Salesforce salary surveys such as the annual Mason Frank Salesforce Salary Survey.

Talk to recruiters:

Recruiters can be a valuable resource for understanding the job market and finding opportunities. Reach out to recruiters who specialize in placing Salesforce administrators to learn more about the current job market and what you can do to increase your chances of finding a job. Note that there are many recruiters who utilize LinkedIn heavily. If you add a Salesforce.com Certification to your LinkedIn Profile, then be prepared to start getting inquires in your LinkedIn Inbox. **Make sure that your LinkedIn profile is up to date prior to adding your certification to your profile. You will 1000% have recruiters reviewing your profile from the day you add your certification details. Be sure to make a good first impression by having all of your other profile related details well-polished.**

2.3. Understanding the Necessary Qualifications and Certifications

As stated above: There are several certifications offered by Salesforce.com, but if you are looking to become a Salesforce Administrator, then you should target getting your Salesforce Certified Administrator credential. You may choose to start with the Salesforce Associate (if you have some experience with Salesforce as an end user), but ultimately most employers are going to want to see that you have the Administrator Certification.

2.3.1. Salesforce Associate

We are not going to focus too much on the Salesforce Associate Certification here, but you should be aware of it, and if you have experience on the Salesforce.com platform, it is definitely worth considering.

Here is what Salesforce says about the Salesforce Associate Certification:

> "The Salesforce Associate certification is designed for individuals who have a fundamental awareness of how an integrated CRM platform solves the challenge of connecting departments and customer data, and who may have up to 6 months of Salesforce user experience. Understanding reporting, user administration, sharing, customization, and data management at a foundational level is also beneficial, but technical expertise is not required."

 Check out Salesforce Certified Associate Credential on Trailhead the for more details.

Note that the Salesforce Associate credential is the most entry-level certification available from Salesforce. Having this certification alone may not be enough to land a job as an Administrator, but it could possibly help you get a job as a Junior Admin. Either way, the process of taking the exam, and the knowledge that you will learn along the way, will no doubt be a great steppingstone on your path toward obtaining your Admin Certification and beginning your new career.

2.3.2. Salesforce Certified Administrator

The Salesforce Certified Administrator credential is designed for individuals who wish to demonstrate their knowledge and proficiency with Salesforce. This certification covers a variety of topics such as data modeling, security settings, reporting, and dashboard configuration. Upon successful completion of the certification exam, applicants are eligible to become a Salesforce professional administrator and have all of the information necessary to maintain and administer a company's cloud-based CRM system. The certification is valid for two years and must be renewed in order to keep one's credentials active. Additionally, the certification may be used to demonstrate competency in business and market specific process automation solutions.

The best-selling Salesforce Administrator Certification Course in the world.

THE COMPLETE SALESFORCE CERTIFIED ADMINISTRATOR COURSE WITH CHATGPT

2.3.3. Commonly asked questions about the Salesforce.com Administrator Certification Exam:

What is the Salesforce Administrator Certification Exam?
The Salesforce Certified Administrator Certification Exam is designed to measure your knowledge and competence in the Salesforce platform.

What is the format of the exam?
The exam is a multiple-choice/multiple-select format. Meaning that each question is presented as multiple choice but may also have multiple answers. For example: The questions may read "select all that apply in _____ scenario," and the test taker would be expected to choose all the correct answers.

How many questions are on the exam?
There are 60 questions and 5 non-scored questions.

How long is the exam?
You will have 105 minutes to complete 60 questions and 5 non-scored questions.

What is the passing score for the exam?
The passing score is 65%. So, you'll need to get at least 39 out of 60 questions correct.

What is the cost of the exam?
There is a $200 registration fee, plus taxes (if required by local law).

How do I register for the exam?
You may take the exam in person at a testing center or online, but either way the exam is proctored. If you choose to take the exam online, you will be remotely proctored via webcam. You can register for an On-Site Proctored Exam by visiting Kryterion's website to find a testing center located near you (the website address is: https://www.kryterion.com/Locate-Test-Center/). if you wish to schedule an Online Proctored Exam, you may do so by going to WebAssessor (website address: www.webassessor.com/salesforce). Note that if you are planning to do the online proctoring then you will want to plan ahead to make sure that your computer setup and external webcam are configured correctly before your scheduled date/time of the exam.

What is the recommended experience level for taking the exam?
Salesforce recommends a combination of hands-on experience, training course completion, Trailhead trails, and self-study in the areas listed in the Exam Outline section of the Salesforce Administrator Exam study guide. We would also recommend considering outside exam prep activities by third parties. Udemy.com and other online training platforms offer a variety of content. We would recommend checking out Mike Wheeler's courses on Udemy. Mike is by far one of the most influential Salesforce.com trainers on the internet. He has helped hundreds of thousands of people obtain their dream of growing their career as a Salesforce.com Professional.

You will probably get the best results when learning through a variety of different content types and learning experiences. You can listen to lectures from people like Mike Wheeler and do the practice activities, as well as hands-on TrailHead Activities. There are other noteworthy resources out there like: Focus On Force, and SFDC99.com.

How often is the exam updated?
The exam is updated on an annual basis.

Are there any prerequisites for taking the exam?
There are no official prerequisites that are required before taking the exam. It is however recommended that you have some experience using Salesforce.com before taking the admin exam. You can certainly know nothing about Salesforce today and still be able to pass the exam within the next 3 to 6 months if you dedicate yourself fully to pursuing it.

What topics are covered on the exam?
The Salesforce Administrator Certification Exam covers a wide range of topics related to the administration and configuration of Salesforce. Some of the specific topics that may be covered on the exam include:

1. User setup and management
2. Security and access
3. Customization of objects, fields, record types, and page layouts
4. Workflow and process automation
5. Reports and dashboards
6. Data management
7. Mobile app configuration
8. AppExchange app installation and management
9. Lightning Experience configuration and management
10. Health checks and performance monitoring

It's important to note that this is not an exhaustive list of all the topics that may be covered on the exam. It's always a good idea to review the exam outline and study materials provided by Salesforce to get a complete understanding of what will be covered on the exam.

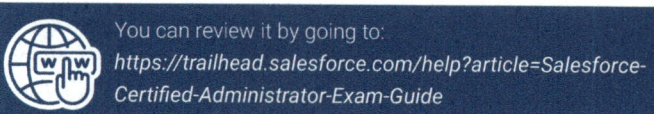

You can review it by going to:
https://trailhead.salesforce.com/help?article=Salesforce-Certified-Administrator-Exam-Guide

How can I prepare for the Salesforce Admin Exam?

There are several steps you can take to prepare for the Salesforce Admin Exam:

1. **Familiarize yourself with the exam content:**
   The Salesforce Admin Exam covers a wide range of topics including user management, data management, security and access, and reporting and analytics. Make sure you have a good understanding of each of these areas.

2. **Review the exam objectives:**
   The exam objectives outline the specific knowledge and skills that will be tested on the exam. Use these objectives to guide your study and make sure you are focusing on the right areas.

3. **Practice with sample questions:**
   There are many resources available online that provide sample questions and practice exams. These can help you get a feel for the types of questions you can expect to see on the exam and can help you identify areas where you need to focus your studying. **A Word of Caution Regarding Practice Exams;** make sure that you are utilizing exam preparation content from reputable sources. There are many "practice tests" on the internet, and many of them can lead you astray. Remember that the exam is conceptual. It's not designed to test your knowledge of any particular facts, figures, or vocabulary but rather to test your knowledge of all the concepts collectively. Do you know enough about how all the concepts impact one another to be able to design the best solution within a company's Salesforce Org? Practice exams can be a good tool, but I would recommend not placing too much weight in them.

4. **Use Salesforce's training resources:**
   Salesforce provides a variety of training resources, including online courses, instructor-led training, and certification study guides. These

resources can help you gain a deeper understanding of the topics covered on the exam and can help you prepare for the exam.

5. **Consider third-party content:**
   There are several courses available that can help you prepare for the Salesforce Admin Exam. These courses often provide a more structured approach to studying and can help you stay focused and on track as you prepare for the exam.

SCAN ME

We would strongly recommend checking out Mike Wheeler's Salesforce Certification Training content

6. **Take care of yourself:**
   It's important to take care of yourself while preparing for the exam. Make sure you get enough sleep, eat well, and take breaks to keep yourself refreshed and focused. As a good friend once told me, "You could read through the entire bible in a week, but you may not get a lot out of it." Early on in your studies you may need to take the content in smaller chunks so that you can truly understand the meaning of each section. You may need to take mental breaks to prevent cognitive overload and watch some of the videos over or do some of the exercises more than once. This is normal! Don't get overwhelmed and quit if you don't understand something the first time through the content. Like a great athlete, repetition in your training will lead to victory! Give yourself permission to repeat the content with small breaks in between, and don't give up!

Are there any study materials or resources available during the exam?
No, there are no study materials or resources available during the Salesforce admin exam. The exam is designed to test your knowledge and skills, and you will not be allowed to use any outside materials or resources during the exam. It is important to make sure you are fully prepared before you take the exam.

Can I retake the exam if I don't pass?
Yes, if you do not pass the Salesforce Certified Administrator Certification Exam on your first attempt you can retake it. Each time you take the exam, you will be presented with a

different set of questions. To ensure that you are fully prepared and have the best chance of success, it is recommended to thoroughly prepare by studying the official self-study guide from Salesforce and taking practice exams from reputable sources.

It's also worth noting that there is a retake fee of $100 for each additional time you need to take the exam.

After receiving my Salesforce Administrator Certification, how do I maintain it and ensure that it doesn't expire?

Your certification must be maintained. Salesforce requires that individuals complete the Salesforce Administrator Maintenance Modules on Trailhead each year. There is no cost to completing the maintenance modules, and this annual activity helps ensure that you stay up to date on new Salesforce product releases.

Landing the Right Job

3.1.   Understanding How Different Companies Use Salesforce

In order to understand what types of Salesforce.com administration jobs are available, it's perhaps best to first consider the primary ways that various companies use Salesforce. Ultimately, as a Salesforce.com professional, you would be working for a company to support their Salesforce Org in whatever way they choose to use you.

Salesforce.com administration jobs encompass a wide range of roles, with job functions including but not limited to basic system admin functions like user management, data administration, building custom Salesforce apps, helping with reporting/dashboarding, and performing various process related configurations. Many companies are seeking a Salesforce.com admin who will perform some variety of all these functions. However, the individual Salesforce.com job is largely dependent on the needs of the individual company. Some salesforce jobs have more of a focus on specific areas like supporting the company's Sales Organization or Service Teams; while others may be looking for someone who can support the company's needs across all departments. Salesforce is widely used across a variety of different industries. Some companies have built apps on the Salesforce platform that serve their industry specific niche. These industry specific custom apps may be utilized to support a company's internal operations, exposed to their customers through a Salesforce Customer Experience Community or exposed to their partners through a Salesforce Partner Experience Community.

Lastly, there is a category of Salesforce.com admin jobs that are there to in some way support Salesforce partners. There are two primary types of Salesforce.com partners:

1. **Salesforce Consultants**

   Salesforce consultants provide clients with guidance for utilizing the Salesforce platform. They can offer expertise in designing, developing, and deploying applications within a company's Salesforce environment. They are responsible for understanding a client's business objectives and translating those into a viable solution using the Salesforce platform. Consultants also provide training to customers on how to use the Salesforce platform, as well as advice on best practices and strategies for utilizing it to meet their objectives. Consulting companies need Salesforce admins to assist in implementing solutions for their customers and providing ongoing customer support.

2. **ISV Partners (or Independent Software Vendors)**

   Salesforce ISV Partners develop custom applications that extend the capabilities of the Salesforce platform. ISV Partners leverage the Salesforce platform and its APIs to create various custom solutions for businesses and then sell these solutions either through the Salesforce AppExchange or as White Labeled SaaS products. ISV Partners need Salesforce Administrators to support their customers and internal operations with tasks such as helping clients with their data migration, user provisioning, training and technical support services, and other ongoing maintenance and support services to keep the system running smoothly.

Recap of Potential Types of Companies Looking to Hire Salesforce Admins:

To quickly recap, below are all the types of employers looking to hire Salesforce.com Administrators:

✦ Companies that need to support their internal operations

✦ Companies that want to create ways to streamline how they interact with their customers

✦ Companies that want to create ways to streamline how they interact with their partners

✦ Consulting Companies that support the implementation of various Salesforce Solutions for their customers

✦ Software Companies (ISV Partners) that build SaaS software on the Salesforce.com platform and sell their offerings through the Salesforce.com App Exchange or as a Whitelabel solution and need to perform the implementation and provide ongoing application support to their customers

3.2. Why Consider Company Type or Industry When Reviewing Salesforce Jobs?

Beyond the obvious need for a certification, much of getting a Salesforce job is convincing someone to hire you. Much of their decision-making process is based on their degree of confidence that you can do the job. Perhaps you are new to Salesforce but you have extensive experience in some particular industry. If you can convey this correctly, then you may be able to relate to the interviewer at this level.

Think of it this way... Let's say 50% of being a good Salesforce.com Administrator is the ability to perform configurations and other functions in Salesforce, and let's say the other 50% is your ability to understand the internal workings of the business so you can adequately access the needs within any situation and make good recommendations. Although Salesforce.com Administration may be new to you, you may have a great level of knowledge from your background in sales, service, marketing, or some specific industry. If you can leverage your background to help convince an interviewer that you already possess a baseline knowledge of their industry or sales processes, etc., then you are sending a powerful message deep into their brain that is telling them that you may be a natural fit for the position they are trying to fill since you can relate at a level deeper than just the technical aspects of Salesforce.

Explore Salesforce Company Management Software By Industry

Automotive	Communications	Consumer Goods	Education
Energy & Utilities	Financial Services	Government	Healthcare & Life Sciences
Manufacturing	Media	Nonprofit	Retail
Technology	Travel Transportation & Hospitality		

SCAN ME

3.3.   Technical Skills Alone
May Not Be Enough

Being able to do the technical functions of a Salesforce.com Administrator is only going to get you halfway there. The good news is you may already have some of the skills required for the other non-technical half of the job, and if not, you can definitely learn the other half of the skills you need while working in a Salesforce.com role. The only bad news is that in order to work in the role, so that you are in a position that allows you to learn these non-technical skills, you have to first convince someone to hire you. This is obviously the biggest challenge when you are getting your first ever Salesforce.com job. This will get easier over time once you have experience, but **how do you overcome this hurdle initially?** To start with, let's try to better understand the soft skills required to be a good Salesforce.com Administrator.

Salesforce has since updated their Administrator Trailhead page so that it no longer lists out the soft skills required, but at one point in the past they had listed the "General Business Skills" needed for Salesforce.com Administrators. They specifically broke down by percentage the "foundational and soft skills most frequently requested by employers looking to fill the Salesforce admin role."

3.3.1.   Most Requested Soft Skills for a
Salesforce.com Administrator:

48%	37%	30%
Communication	Organization	Problem-solving/ Troubleshooting

23%	20%
Project Management	Attention to Detail

Notice that 48% of employers looking to hire a Salesforce.com Administrator specifically listed communication skills as a desired soft skill. It's quite interesting that Salesforce Admins are often thought of as being only an IT/technical role, and in many ways it is a highly technical role; however, as technology has evolved, the needs and expectations of companies' IT departments have dramatically changed as well. A Salesforce.com Administrator is an interesting role because it may report into the IT Department but it may also report to someone within the Business. Either way, when business decisions are being made, a Salesforce Admin often has a seat at the metaphorical table. Many times, this is due to the business's desire to have their Salesforce Professional in the conversations to help assess how technically feasible different ideas may be, or at least to be present in the conversations so that the Admin can better understand what problems the business is trying to solve. Companies are seeking individuals who can optimize technical processes in Salesforce but also have the communication skills to help drive the process forward. Many of these soft skills can be learned, so don't lose heart if these things don't come naturally to you at first, just be aware that technical ability is only part of what is needed to excel as a Salesforce Admin, and with time you can grow your overall skillset.

Consider the "Most Requested Soft Skills for a Salesforce.com Administrator" listed above. Which of these skills do you feel you may already have experience with? Be sure to leverage the related soft skills that come naturally to you by highlighting them on your resume.

Tools To Create Stunning Resume

https://www.datasciencecompany.com/create-a-stunning-resume-with-canva-a-comprehensive-guide/

JANE DOE

Salesforce Professional

As a highly motivated and experienced Salesforce Administrator, I am seeking a challenging role that will enable me to leverage my skills and expertise in managing and supporting Salesforce systems to drive business growth and enhance customer experience. With a proven track record of successfully managing Salesforce systems, I am dedicated to maximizing the full potential of this platform through effective system configuration, data management, and user adoption strategies. I am eager to bring my strong technical aptitude and customer-focused mindset to an organization that values innovation, collaboration, and continuous improvement, and where I can make a significant impact by ensuring the smooth operation and continuous improvement of Salesforce systems.

CONTACT

- hello@reallygreatsite.com
- +123-456-7890
- Franklin, TN

CERTIFICATIONS

- Salesforce Certified Administrator
- Salesforce Certified Advanced Administrator
- Salesforce Certified Platform App Builder

TECH SKILLS

- Flow Builder
- Salesforce Data Loader and Data Import Wizard
- Salesforce Reporting and Dashboards
- Salesforce integration with third-party systems

WORK EXPERIENCE

SALESFORCE ADMIN   May 2018 - Present
Warren & Spencer

- Managed and maintained Salesforce systems, including user management, data quality, and security settings.
- Created and customized reports and dashboards to provide insights into key performance metrics and sales pipeline.
- Collaborated with sales and marketing teams to optimize lead management and conversion processes.
- Conducted user training and support to ensure maximum adoption and utilization of Salesforce systems.

SALESFORCE DEVELOPER   Sept 2016 - May 2018
Wardiere Inc.

- Designed and developed custom Salesforce solutions using Apex, Visualforce, and Lightning Components.
- Integrated Salesforce systems with third-party applications and platforms such as Marketo and Hubspot.
- Collaborated with business stakeholders to gather and document requirements and provide technical solutions to meet their needs.
- Conducted code reviews and provided feedback to other developers to ensure high-quality code.

EDUCATION

CORNELL UNIVERSITY, Ithaca, NY   2011 - 2016
Bachelor of Science in Business Administration
- Honors: cum laude (GPA 3.8/4.0)

Writing An Attention Grabbing Resume

Writing an attention-grabbing resume and cover letter can be a bit of a challenge. But with these 8 tips, you'll be sure to make an impression!

4.1.　Use a Resume Template

Starting with a resume template is probably the best way to get a good resume layout. You want to find a resume layout that is both functional and has a little personality. It doesn't have to be too fancy. Using a template can also help make sure your resume is well structured and easy to read. Use clear headings, bullet points, and an appropriate length. Ideally limit your resume to one page if possible. In order to neatly fit more content into a single page, you may want to consider using a resume template that has a sidebar. Consider using section headings to better structure your content. For example, you may want to include the following sections: Profile, Objective, Contact, Core Competencies, Work Experience, Education, Certifications, etc. You don't necessarily need to have all of these, but this may serve as a good idea of where to start (a good two column template from Microsoft Word will go a long way to get you started).

4.2.　Use Occam's Razor

Occam's Razor, also known as the principle of parsimony, is a philosophical and scientific principle that states that the simplest explanation is likely to be correct. It suggests that among competing hypotheses, the one with the fewest assumptions should be selected. This means looking for an answer or solution that makes the fewest assumptions and is easy to comprehend.

How do you apply this to your resume? KEEP IT SIMPLE! Less is more. **Remember that the purpose of your resume is to get an interview.** Your resume is to get you in front of someone in an interview so that they can ask you questions. Don't try to make your resume so inclusive of everything you have ever done. Let them ask questions. If your resume is too full of irrelevant details, then you will likely not even get to the interview process.

4.3.   Focus on your accomplishments rather than just listing duties performed in each job you've had

When it comes to writing a resume, it's important to understand that potential employers are not just interested in the job titles you have held or the duties you have performed in your previous roles. Instead, they want to know how your work experience has contributed to your personal and professional growth, and how you have made a difference in the organizations you have worked for. To make your resume stand out from the pile of others, you should focus on your accomplishments.

An accomplishment is a specific achievement or result that you have produced during your employment. It's the outcome of your hard work, dedication, and expertise. When describing your work experience on your resume, you should highlight your accomplishments instead of just listing your duties. By doing so, you show potential employers what you can bring to their organization and how you can make a positive impact on their business.

To effectively showcase your accomplishments, you should use strong action verbs and provide quantifiable results. For example, instead of saying Managed a team of sales representatives, you could say Led a team of sales representatives that achieved a 20% increase in revenue over a six-month period. By providing specific, measurable results, you demonstrate your ability to produce tangible outcomes and add value to the organizations you have worked for.

Remember, your resume is your marketing tool, and you want to use it to show potential employers how you can benefit their business. By focusing on your accomplishments, you can make a powerful impression and stand out from the competition.

Highlight skills that are relevant to the job you're applying for.

Show how they're transferable and make connections to other experiences or successes whenever possible. If some of your Work History doesn't apply to the position that you are applying for, then minimize it. Don't submit a resume with multiple bullet points below a previous job when those bulleted points don't relate to the job you are applying for. Furthermore, specifically think about how that previous job role would relate, and under that job description only list on your resume what is transferable to the job you are applying for. Always be honest about what skills you possess and what your experience has been, but selectively share only what is relevant. Too many non-relevant details will only distract from the relevant qualifications you want to highlight.

Always consider the underlying skills that are required to perform a task, and highlight the skills that are transferable.

For Example: There is no need outline all the duties you held while in your college restaurant job. Instead, just list the aspect of your restaurant service job in a way that it relates to a Salesforce Admin role.

For example, you may say something like:

> "Working at Chilies was a great experience to refine my customer service skills while: exercising attention to detail, optimizing my time management through daily incremental process improvements, and further learning the value of teamwork."

Articulating your experience in such a way will help the interviewer draw some parallels between your past seemingly unrelated job, and the skills needed to perform the current Salesforce Admin job. In addition, by articulating your experience in such a way that focuses on the skills vs. the tasks of a role, it goes well beyond the obvious and will demonstrate that you have the ability to draw deeper connections and correlations. This deeper level of thinking and pattern recognition is a great trait for a Salesforce.com Administrator!

4.4. Use strong action verbs throughout your resume

Using strong action verbs throughout your resume is an essential component of effective resume writing. Action verbs bring your achievements to life and make your resume more dynamic and engaging. They show potential employers that you are an active participant in your work and have a track record of success. By using action verbs, you also communicate your skills and abilities more clearly and concisely, which can help you stand out from other applicants.

When choosing action verbs for your resume, consider the specific achievements and results you want to highlight. For example, if you developed a new product, you might use verbs such as created, innovated, or designed. If you achieved a sales target, you might use verbs such as exceeded, surpassed, or outperformed. If you initiated a new program, you might use verbs such as launched, established, or implemented.

It's important to use a variety of action verbs throughout your resume, rather than repeating the same ones over and over. This can help keep your resume fresh and engaging and demonstrate your versatility as a candidate. Additionally, using active voice (e.g., Developed a new marketing campaign) rather than passive voice (e.g., A new marketing campaign was developed by me) can make your achievements sound more impressive and impactful.

In summary, using strong action verbs throughout your resume can make a big difference in how potential employers perceive you as a candidate. By choosing specific, impactful verbs and using active voice, you can showcase your achievements and skills in a compelling way and increase your chances of landing the job you want.

4.5. Tailor your resume to the specific position you're applying for

When applying for a job, it's essential to tailor your resume to the specific position you're applying for. This means taking the time to carefully review the job description and requirements, and then adjusting your resume to highlight the qualifications and experiences that make you the best fit for the job. By doing so, you demonstrate to potential employers that you have taken the time to understand their needs and requirements, and that you are committed to the position.

To tailor your resume effectively, you should start by reviewing the job description and identifying the key skills, qualifications, and experiences that the employer is looking for. Then, you can adjust your resume to highlight your own relevant skills and experiences. For example, if the job requires experience with a particular software program, you can emphasize your own experience with that program. Or, if the job requires strong leadership skills, you can highlight your experience managing teams or leading projects.

It's also important to use keywords from the job description throughout your resume. Many employers use applicant tracking systems (ATS) to scan resumes for keywords that match the job requirements. By using relevant keywords in your resume, you increase your chances of getting past the ATS and into the hands of the hiring manager.

In summary, tailoring your resume to the specific position you're applying for is essential to stand out from other candidates. By highlighting your unique qualifications and experiences that align with the job requirements, and using relevant keywords, you can demonstrate why you are the best fit for the job and increase your chances of landing an interview.

4.6.   Check for typos or errors

When it comes to writing a resume, attention to detail is crucial, especially when applying for Salesforce jobs. A single mistake or typo on your resume can cost you a job opportunity, as it may suggest a lack of attention to detail or a lack of care in your work. Employers in the Salesforce industry expect candidates to have a high level of attention to detail, as this is a critical skill in working with complex data and systems. Therefore, it's essential to take the time to proofread your resume carefully, checking for spelling errors, grammar mistakes, and formatting inconsistencies. You may also want to ask a trusted friend or mentor to review your resume to catch any errors you may have missed. By presenting a polished, error-free resume, you demonstrate your attention to detail and increase your chances of getting hired for a Salesforce job.

4.7. Add some subtle color for personality!

Don't be afraid to showcase your unique skills and interests in a creative way! I have worked in large companies, and I've seen hundreds of resumes cross my desk when hiring Salesforce.com professionals. There have been multiple times when I'd be given a stack of resumes (either literally or electronically) and we would have only a couple of hours to go through 40 to 60 applicants and determine who would advance to the next round. This is a lot of stress as a hiring manager who has been given a short time to review a lot of resumes in order to find just the right candidate.

If a resume contained obvious mistakes, had wall to wall text, or crookedly stapled papers that didn't line up... then they were out. From what remained, the applications were then filtered again based on some general certification requirements or relatable experience criteria, and from those, any resumes that generally speaking seemed boring would go to the bottom of the stack. You want your resume to stand out for all the right reasons. Hiring managers are people too. They need to believe that you're qualified and that they can trust you but they also like to see some personality. Consider having a simple splash of subtle color in the header, background color under your sidebar, or maybe even include a professional headshot image, etc... these subtle things will go a long way in making your resume stand out in a sea of boring black and white resumes.

4.7.1. Resume Summary

A well-crafted resume is an essential tool for any job seeker. Following these tips will help you create a tailored, professional-looking resume that will stand out from the competition and make a great impression on potential employers. With good organization and proper formatting, your resume can showcase your skills and accomplishments in an easy-to-read layout. Put the extra effort into making sure your resume stands out from the rest and you'll be sure to make a memorable impact!

Remember that the purpose of your resume is to get an interview.

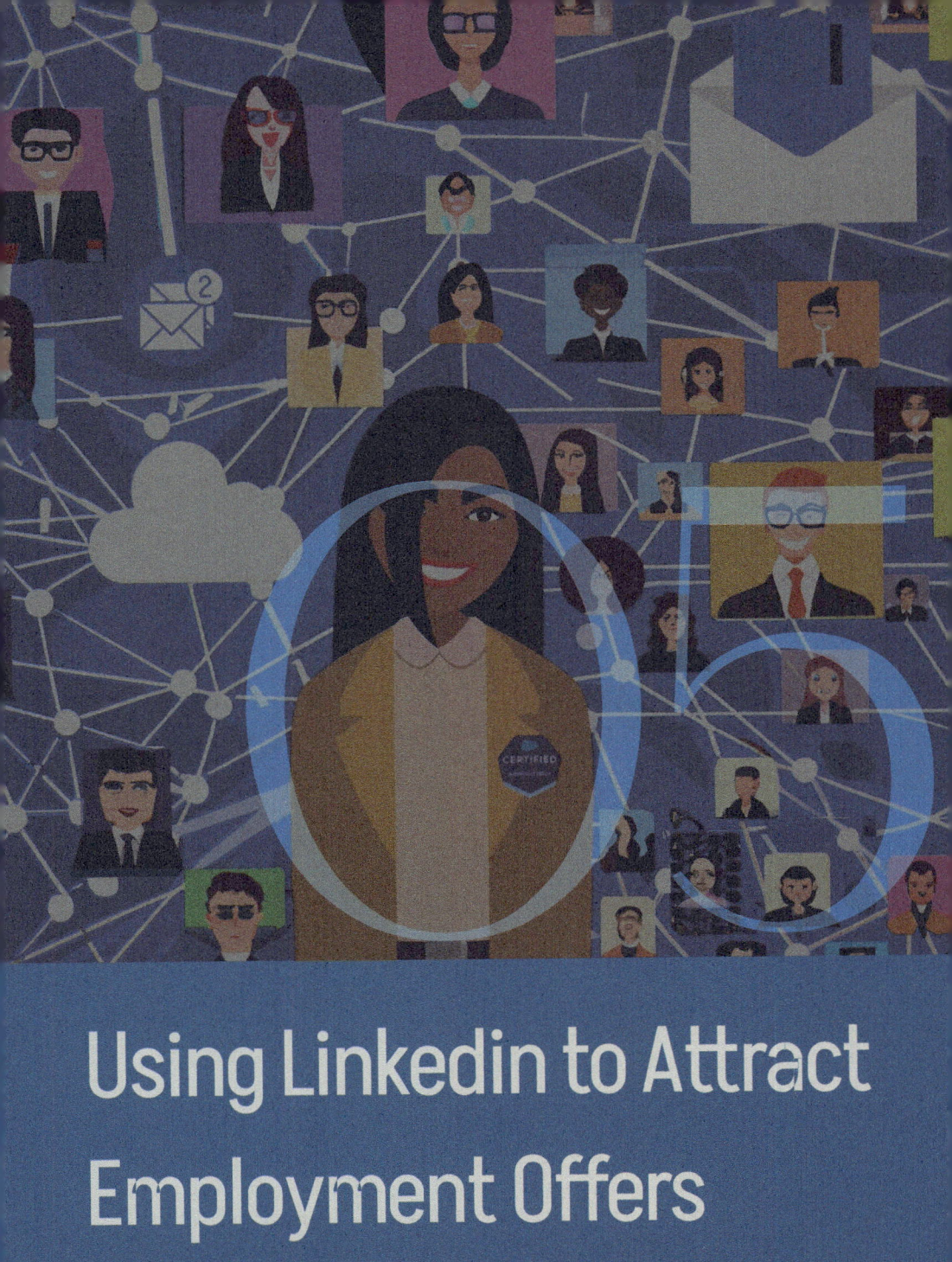

Using Linkedin to Attract Employment Offers

5.1.   LinkedIn Best Practices

Now that your resume has been updated, it's time to update your LinkedIn Profile. As you are probably already aware, LinkedIn is a professional social network that connects millions of professionals from around the world. It allows users to network with each other, find jobs, and stay up to date on industry news. Your LinkedIn Profile should basically be a reflection of the content found on your resume. Updating your LinkedIn profile is an important way to ensure that you are presenting the best version of yourself to potential employers and networking connections.

Here are some best practices for updating your LinkedIn profile:

Use a professional profile picture:

01   Choose a profile picture that is clear and professional. Avoid using a photo that is too casual or that includes other people.

Write a clear and concise headline:

02   Your headline should be a brief summary of your professional identity. It should include your current job title and a few key skills or areas of expertise.

Update your work experience:

03   Make sure to list all of your relevant work experience, including your current job. Include details about your responsibilities and achievements at each job. Just like you did on your resume, you should minimize any details about current or past jobs that don't relate to your desired type of employment.

Add your education:

04   List all of your educational qualifications, including the degree you received and the name of the institution.

Link your Trailhead to your LinkedIn:

05   Linking your Trailhead Account to your LinkedIn profile is a great way to showcase your Salesforce certifications, badges, and accomplishments. It will also make it easier for potential employers or recruiters to find your profile and get an overview of your skills and experience. By linking your Trailhead account to your LinkedIn profile, you are making sure that the information is up-to-date and accurate, allowing recruiters and employers to get an accurate snapshot of who you are as a professional. Of course, if you are going to do this, then be sure to stay engaged on your Trailhead account to rack up Trailhead points and add additional badges.

Include any relevant skills:

06 Add any skills that you have that are relevant to the Salesforce.com Administrator role. Review the previous section titled "Most Requested Soft Skills for a Salesforce.com Administrator." Include any soft skills that you have. Also include industry related skills like: "Salesforce.com," "CRM," or "Analytics." When considering prior positions, always consider the underlying skills that are required to perform a task, and highlight those skills that are transferable. You may also consider asking current or previous colleagues to consider endorsing you for said skills if you feel it's appropriate to do so.

Connect with others:

07 LinkedIn is a networking platform, so it's important to build connections with other professionals. Connect with people you know and consider joining relevant groups to expand your network.

Use keywords:

08 Include relevant keywords in your profile to make it easier for people to find you when searching for specific skills or industries. Consider sprinkling in keyword to your Headline, Title, About, and Experience sections. Consider general terms like "Certified Salesforce Professional" or "Certified Salesforce Administrator" within your headline.

Customize your URL:

09 Make it easy for people to find your LinkedIn profile by customizing your URL to include your name or a professional handle.

Review and proofread:

10 Before you save any updates to your profile, be sure to review and proofread everything to ensure that it is accurate and free of errors.

When Adding Salesforce Certifications: update LinkedIn profile (as needed):

11 You should ensure your LinkedIn Profile is up to date before adding your Salesforce.com certification credential. You will end up adding your Salesforce Certifications to the "Licenses and certifications" section of your LinkedIn Profile. There are a number of recruiters who subscribe to LinkedIn's Premium Talent Solutions services. They specifically search for people with Salesforce Certifications, and you will most likely get recruiters reaching out to you as soon as you update your LinkedIn Profile with your certification details. Make the best impression possible by updating the rest of your profile's details before adding additional certifications.

5.2. Amplify Your LinkedIn Profile: 6 Key Tools You Should Be Using

In addition to the general overall best practices that we just covered, consider these six standout tools that can aid in keeping your LinkedIn profile updated and engaging:

5.2.1. LinkedIn's Built-In Profile Strength Meter

Maximizing Your Potential with LinkedIn's Profile Strength Meter

Before we jump into external tools, it's important to acknowledge the usefulness of LinkedIn's own Profile Strength Meter. The Profile Strength Meter measures the completeness and robustness of a user's profile. It evaluates various elements such as the profile photo, headline, summary, work experience, education, skills, and endorsements. Based on this evaluation, it determines the profile's strength,

Profile Strength

All-Star

Looks like there is room for improvement, right?

Actually, this is the highest level strength you can attain on your LinkedIn profile.

Share your profile ›

ranging from "Just Beginning" to "All-Star," the highest level of profile strength. The meter's dynamic nature is a remarkable feature - as you add or update information, it recalculates in real time to provide instant feedback.

But the Profile Strength Meter is not just a gauge; it's a guide too. It identifies areas of your profile that are lacking and prompts you to add missing elements such as certifications, languages, or skills. By following its cues, users can easily ensure that they are utilizing all the areas LinkedIn has to offer. This allows users to fully highlight their professional journey and unique skill set.

Despite its simplicity, the Profile Strength Meter's value should not be underestimated. Its use has the potential to significantly elevate your LinkedIn presence. With a profile that the meter deems strong, you'll likely gain increased visibility and credibility, better showcasing your professional persona to peers, recruiters, and potential employers.

The Profile Strength Meter is a formidable tool within the LinkedIn platform that facilitates the creation of comprehensive and appealing profiles. It's worth taking the time to regularly check in with this tool, fill in any gaps it points out, and move closer to that coveted 'All-Star' status.

5.2.2.   Canva

Power up Your LinkedIn Presence with Canva: An Easy-to-Use Design Tool

A profile with well-designed graphics can stand out amidst the sea of text-based LinkedIn profiles. Canva, an easy-to-use design tool, can help you create eye-catching graphics. Whether it's a custom banner for your profile or an infographic showcasing your skills, Canva has got you covered. With its myriad of templates and intuitive interface, Canva has the resources to help you amplify your LinkedIn profile's visual appeal even if your not a designer.

Canva's primary appeal lies in its sheer simplicity and user-friendly interface. This platform is meticulously designed, keeping in mind both professional designers and those with little to no design experience. Hence, even without a background in graphic design, you can leverage Canva to create stunning visuals that lend a professional touch to your LinkedIn profile.

One of Canva's standout features is its extensive library of templates. These templates span across various categories and designs, providing you with a ready-made foundation to kick-start your creativity. You can select a template that aligns with your vision and modify it as per your needs. This reduces the time and effort you need to invest in creating graphics from scratch.

Moreover, Canva allows for a high degree of customization, enabling you to match your graphics with your personal brand or professional aesthetic. You can experiment with different colors, fonts, and elements until you find the perfect combination that encapsulates your professional persona.

In essence, Canva can be your powerful ally in enhancing your LinkedIn profile. Through captivating and professional visuals, you can not only make your profile more engaging but also convey your story and skills more effectively. Even without a background in design, Canva's easy-to-use platform and a wealth of resources empower you to create compelling graphics, leading to a standout LinkedIn profile. So why not give Canva a shot and let your LinkedIn profile shine brighter?

5.2.3.   Grammarly

Elevate Your LinkedIn Content with Grammarly: Your Personal Writing Assistant

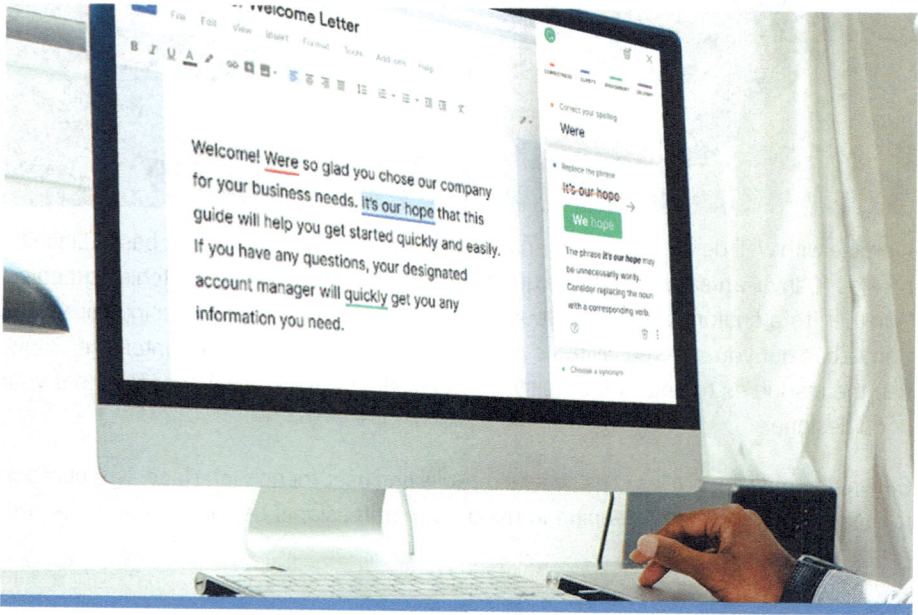

On LinkedIn, the clarity and polish of your written content can greatly influence the impressions you make. Typos, incorrect grammar, or poorly structured sentences can undermine your professional image. That's where Grammarly, a free online writing assistant, comes into play. It aids you in crafting clear, error-free text, which can significantly enhance your LinkedIn communications.

Grammarly is more than just a spell-checker; it's an intelligent tool that checks for contextual spelling mistakes, grammar, punctuation, sentence structure, and even style. Whether you're drafting a captivating summary, detailing your experiences, or crafting an engaging article to share with your network, Grammarly can provide invaluable assistance.

One of the unique features of Grammarly is its real-time feedback. As you type, Grammarly is hard at work underlining potential issues and providing suggestions for improvements. This not only helps you fix errors on the spot, but also aids in improving your writing skills over time.

Grammarly's utility extends beyond just correcting mistakes; it also offers suggestions to make your writing more concise and impactful. For instance, it might suggest replacing a common word with a more specific synonym to enhance your sentence's impact. It can also flag sentences that may come off as too wordy or unclear, helping you refine your communication style.

In summary, Grammarly serves as a powerful tool for any LinkedIn user keen on making a strong professional impression. It ensures your written content is not just error-free, but also clear and engaging. Leveraging Grammarly can help you present yourself more confidently and effectively on LinkedIn, boosting your professional credibility.

5.2.4.   Word Clouds

Boost Your LinkedIn Profile Visibility with Word Clouds

LinkedIn operates on algorithms, with search visibility heavily influenced by the strategic use of relevant keywords. One innovative way to identify these critical keywords is by using Word Clouds, an insightful tool that can bolster your LinkedIn profile's discoverability.

Word Clouds works by analyzing a given text and generating a visual representation of the most frequently used words, with their size correlating to their frequency. This enables you to easily identify and focus on the most prominent terms.

For LinkedIn profile optimization, you can feed Word Clouds with job descriptions, skill lists, or even industry-related articles. The resulting word cloud would then emphasize the terms that are most often used, suggesting the industry-specific keywords that you should consider incorporating into your LinkedIn profile.

By including these identified keywords in your headline, summary, and job descriptions, you increase your profile's chances of appearing in relevant searches by recruiters and industry professionals. This can lead to more connection requests, direct messages, and even job opportunities.

In addition, Word Clouds can help you ensure your language aligns with industry norms, further establishing your credibility and understanding within your field.

In review, Word Clouds is a practical and easy-to-use tool that can enhance the effectiveness of your LinkedIn profile. By helping you identify and incorporate vital keywords, Word Clouds can significantly amplify your profile's visibility, strengthening your professional networking efforts.

5.2.5.   Feedly

Keep Your LinkedIn Profile Dynamic with Feedly: Your Personalized Content Aggregator

A vibrant LinkedIn profile is not just about showcasing your skills and experiences, but also demonstrating your knowledge and engagement in your field. Feedly, a top-notch RSS aggregator, can serve as a valuable resource in this respect, ensuring you're always on top of industry news and trends.

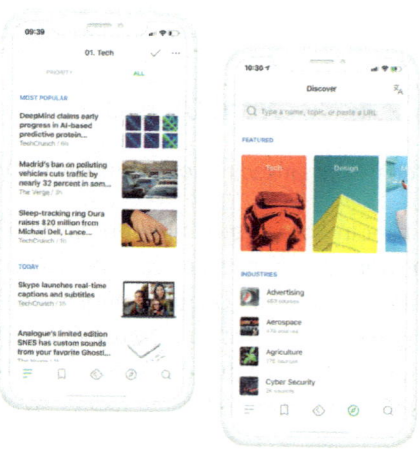

Feedly streamlines your content consumption by consolidating articles and posts from your favorite blogs, news sites, and other sources into a single feed. By catering to your personal interests and professional domain, Feedly provides you with a constant stream of relevant content that you can utilize to boost your LinkedIn profile's dynamism.

One of the effective ways to leverage Feedly's offerings is by regularly sharing industry-specific content on your LinkedIn profile. Not only does this highlight your ongoing engagement with your field, but it also positions you as a knowledgeable professional who is well-versed with the latest trends and developments.

In addition, commenting on such content with your insights and perspectives can further establish your expertise and thought leadership. This level of engagement not only enhances your LinkedIn presence but can also spark meaningful conversations with other professionals in your network, further strengthening your professional relationships.

In summary, Feedly offers a seamless solution to staying abreast with your industry's pulse, thereby aiding you in maintaining a dynamic and relevant LinkedIn profile. By leveraging this tool, you can consistently project your engagement and proficiency in your field, solidifying your standing as a knowledgeable professional.

5.2.6. Jobscan

Amplify Your Job Search with Jobscan: AI-Powered LinkedIn Optimization Tool

In the digital age of recruitment, having a resume and LinkedIn profile that aligns with specific job postings can be a significant advantage. Jobscan, an AI-powered tool, serves precisely this purpose. It optimizes your LinkedIn profile and resume to increase your chances of catching a recruiter's eye and passing through an Applicant Tracking System (ATS).

Jobscan works by comparing a job description with your LinkedIn profile or resume. It analyses the text to identify the frequency and relevance of specific keywords, skills,

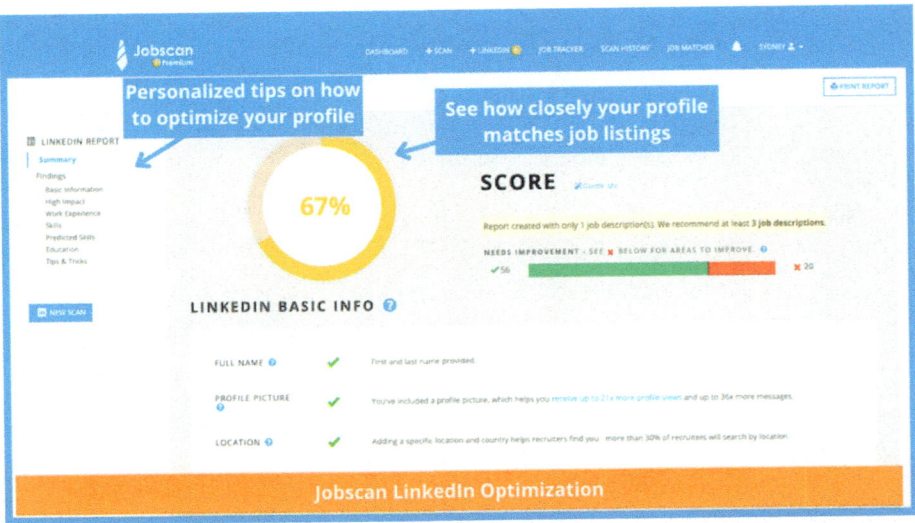

and other vital aspects in the job description. Following this analysis, Jobscan provides personalized recommendations for enhancing your profile or resume to better match the role.

This process is particularly beneficial during a job search. When recruiters use an ATS, they're often filtering candidates based on specific keywords. By tailoring your profile and resume to include these keywords, you significantly improve your chances of making it through the initial ATS screening and getting noticed by recruiters.

Furthermore, Jobscan's suggestions can help you present your skills and experiences in a way that directly resonates with potential employers. This can not only increase your chances of landing an interview but also set the stage for you to demonstrate how well you fit the role during the interview process.

In summary, Jobscan is an invaluable tool for any job seeker aiming to optimize their LinkedIn profile and resume. By utilizing its AI-powered analysis and suggestions, you can position yourself more effectively for specific roles, thereby enhancing your job search efforts.

Conclusion

Keeping your LinkedIn profile updated and engaging is a key step in personal branding and professional networking. With these tools at your disposal, you can significantly simplify the process and make your profile truly shine. Whether you're passively networking, actively job seeking, or just looking to maintain a professional presence online, an optimized LinkedIn profile is your ticket to success. Remember that consistency is key, so make sure to regularly use these tools to keep your profile in tip-top shape.

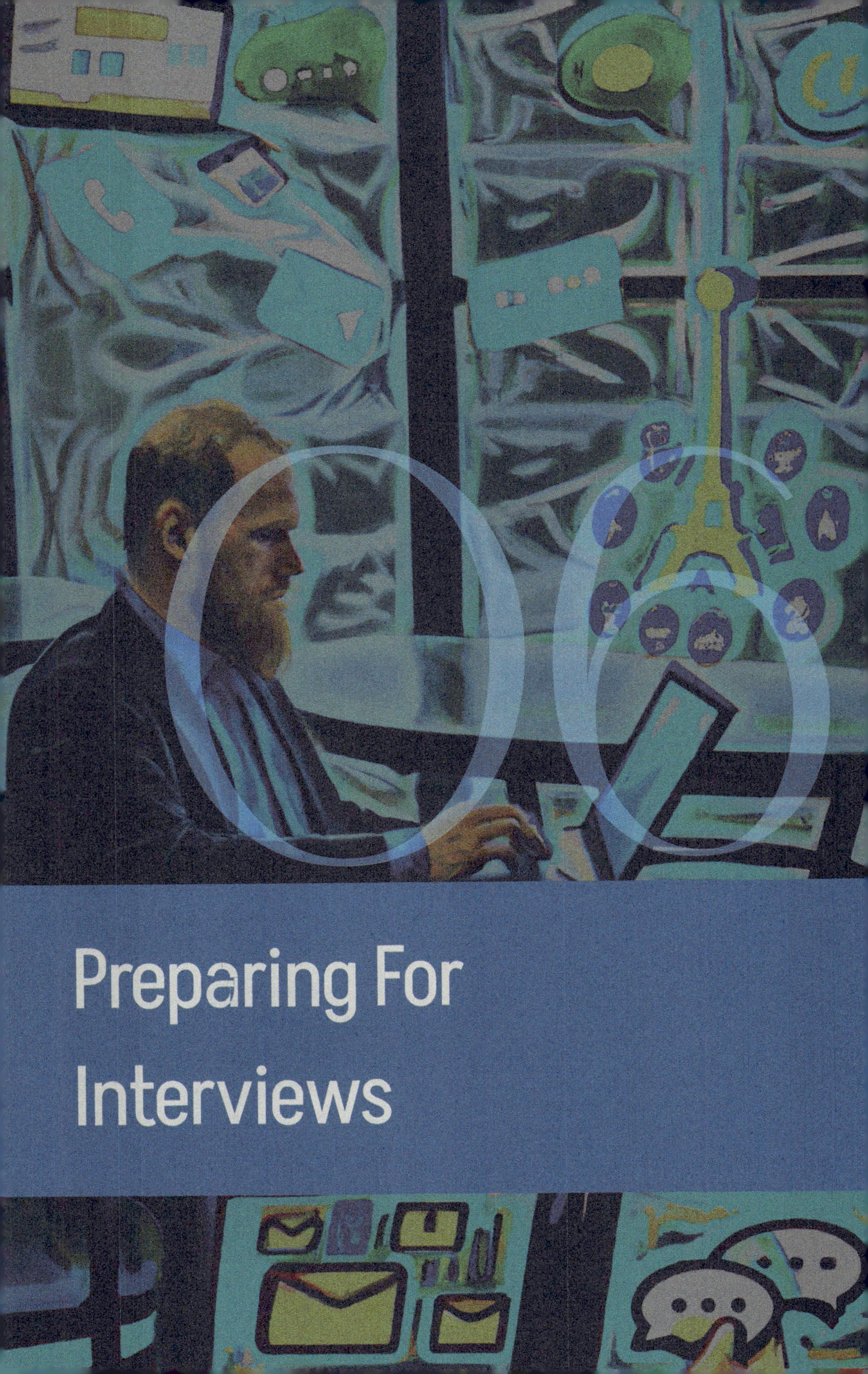

Preparing For
Interviews

Preparation is key to making a good impression at a job interview, and this is especially true for a Salesforce.com Administrator position. Here are some steps you can take to get ready for your interview:

6.1.   Research the company

Make sure to review their website, read about recent news, and keep up with any announcements prior to the interview. Take some time to learn about the company's history, culture, products, and services. This will not only help you understand the business better, but it will also give you some ideas for what questions to ask the interviewer.

6.2.   Visit the location

Visit the place ahead of time if possible to get familiar with the neighborhood and see where you'll be walking or driving to on the day of your interview.

6.3.   Review the job posting

Carefully review the job posting to get a sense of the skills and experience the company is looking for. Make a list of the requirements and think about how your experience, skills, and education make you a good fit for the role.

6.4.   Practice your answers

Anticipate common questions that might be asked in the interview, such as "Tell me about yourself," "Why do you want to work for our company?" and "What are your strengths and weaknesses?" Practice your responses so that you feel confident and comfortable answering these questions.

6.5. Brush up on the latest Salesforce happenings

Make sure you are familiar with the latest features and functionality of the Salesforce platform. Review the changes from the most recent release of Salesforce and be aware of any big upcoming changes. The easiest way to do this is to search out "Salesforce Release Notes Summary" or "Salesforce Release Notes Quick Overview" on Google and YouTube. You can of course also take the time to look through the official Salesforce Release Notes provided by Salesforce, but these tend to be quite long and may be overwhelming to you when you are already utilizing lots of mental space to prepare for your interview. By being aware of the latest and upcoming happenings with the Salesforce platform, you may be able to naturally work some of this information into a conversation during the interview. This can be a great subtle way for you to show that you know your stuff and possibly add value to the company before you even start by making them aware of something they may not have otherwise already known.

6.6. Prepare an elevator pitch

Put together a concise professional summary that you can use in case you're asked to introduce yourself during the interview.

6.7. Come prepared with questions

Have questions ready that will demonstrate your interest in the role, such as inquiries about the team size or organizational structure within the department you would be working in if hired.

You want your questions to be within a conversation naturally. They may answer some of your questions before you even ask. Be thinking about all the company and role specific questions that you would like to know. Don't pepper them with questions as if it was some form of an interrogation. As naturally as possible, ask your questions throughout the interview as it makes sense to do so. If they have a more formalized interview process that doesn't allow for in the moment questions from you, then just go with the flow... they will most likely give you the opportunity to ask your questions before the interview is over.

Below is a list of the type of questions you may want to consider asking. DO NOT take a printed copy of all these questions into an interview. Keep things as conversational as possible and allow the interviewer time to answer one question and complete their thought before throwing more questions their way. Again, it not advised that you go in and ask all these questions. The intent of the list below is to get you thinking about what type of questions you would like to ask. With that said, review the questions below and make a mental list of the questions you would like to ask:

✦ How is Salesforce.com currently being used within the company?

✦ Can you describe the current state of the company's data and how it is being utilized within Salesforce.com?

✦ How does the company plan to utilize Salesforce.com in the future, and how will the role of the Salesforce.com Administrator fit into those plans?

✦ Can you describe the current team structure and how I will be working with other team members if I were in this position?

✦ How does the company handle data migration and integrations with other systems?

✦ Can you describe the company's release management process and how the Salesforce.com Administrator will be involved?

✦ How does the company handle user support and training for Salesforce.com?

✦ Can you describe the current customizations and features that have been implemented within the Salesforce.com platform and how they are being utilized by the company?

✦ Can you describe the company's approach to security and data privacy within Salesforce.com?

✦ How does the company handle ongoing maintenance and updates to the Salesforce.com platform?

- Which business groups have processes supported by Salesforce? (sales, service, marketing, are there custom apps to support other functions?)

- What are some of the biggest problems you are trying to solve that the Salesforce admin role may be assisting with?

- Could you describe the definition of success for this position during the first 90 days? 6 months? or 1 year?

- What are the goals and objectives for this position in the first year? Are there any specific projects that you are targeting to be completed during this timeframe?

- How is the Salesforce Org currently supported? Are there other internal team members or any outside consultants assisting with managing the org?

- What is the size of the team supporting Salesforce?

- How does this team collaborate on projects or initiatives?

- What kind of change management processes are currently in place?

- Are there any company policies or required software validation templates that would impact how changes are deployed in Salesforce?

- How big is the Salesforce Org? How many users? What types of users (sales, service, etc.)?

- Who does this position report to?

- Is this a newly created position? If not, then follow up with a question of: May I ask who occupied the position before and why they chose to leave?

- Can you explain the process of onboarding a new employee?

- What are the major responsibilities for this role?

- Are there any challenges that I should be aware of in this role?

- What type of customer data does this role involve working with and how is it maintained and protected?

- What strategies has your organization implemented to successfully utilize Salesforce?

- "Based on the discussion we have had so far, is there any reason that you would not hire me for this position?" This can be a great question to ask because it gives the interviewer a chance to state any reservations they may have in hiring you, and it gives you a chance to quickly respond to overcome those reservations. It may also help you better understand things about yourself—or your presentation skills) that you can improve before your next interview.

Clearly, you're not going to go into an interview and ask all these questions, but hopefully it gets you thinking about the types of questions you'd like to ask in a given situation.

6.8. Dress professionally

Make sure to choose an outfit appropriate for both the position and company culture; don't forget small details like a firm handshake and good posture!

6.9. Arrive early

Plan ahead so that you have plenty of time to get there before your appointed time; arriving late could send a clear message that you're not prepared or interested in this opportunity!

6.10. Have some stories to tell

Have 2 or 3 stories ready to tell to demonstrate how you've used Salesforce to meet the needs of a business or solve problems in past roles; this will show hiring managers your experience level with the platform as well as your problem-solving abilities. Have these stories rehearsed and ready to tell and look for opportunities to slip them into the conversation as you can, perhaps they will serve as a good answer to one of the interview questions. Try to keep it as conversational as possible. Maybe start by telling a short version of the story and if they are interested elaborate into a longer version based on their questions. It doesn't need to be super scripted but it should cover some basic details such as a problem, a solution, and a result. Below are some tips on how to mentally format your story, and some examples of how to tell your story in both a short and longer version.

6.10.1. Story Format:

Your stories need to be fairly brief, but whether it's a quick story or more detailed version, you should try to be sure your story covers these three simple points:

 Frame up the problem

 Explain what action was taken within Salesforce

 Review the benefits that came from the changes you made. If possible, try to tie the benefits back to more tangible results related to revenue, margin, or compliance.

In an interview, you're going to be expected to be quick on your feet, and you won't have the luxury of reading from your notes to answer questions. Mark Twain once stated: "If I had more time, I would have written a shorter letter." There is something about being concise and effective that is highly valued in the workplace. Remember that 48% of employers have listed communication as a soft skill that they wish to see in a Salesforce. com Administrator. Part of communicating is simply taking the time beforehand to be prepared. I'm not advising that you try to stick to some script, but I would highly suggest to prep your story so that you have no issues clearly explaining what problem you solved, what you did to solve it, and what the outcome/benefits were. Give this section some serious thought. Have you had any Salesforces successes that you would be able to share as stories in an interview?

Below is an example of a story that I shared in interviews early on in my salesforce journey. This is before I had anything experience in Salesforce.com to lean on. My only initial story was that of some simple reports and dashboards, but I was able to leverage this story to help obtain a role in supporting a company's Salesforce Org, and that led to additional wins and better stories to tell.

Short Story Example:

> "I worked for a company in a sales related role and discovered an issue with opportunities falling through the cracks. I was able to use native Salesforce. com Reports and Dashboards to highlight any opportunity that would potentially fall through the cracks for each individual sales rep. By making sure that no opportunities were getting missed, the company picked up an additional $3.4mil in sales as a direct result of these simple changes."

NOTICE HOW THIS SHORT STORY FITS INTO THE FOLLOWING FORMAT:

Framing up the problem:

01   I worked for a company in a Sales related role and discovered an issue with opportunities falling through the cracks.

Explain what action was taken within Salesforce:

02   I was able to use native Salesforce.com Reports and Dashboards to highlight any opportunity that would potentially fall through the cracks for each individual sales rep.

Review the benefits that came from the changes:

03   By making sure that no opportunities were getting missed, the company picked up an additional $3.4mil in sales as a direct result of these simple changes.

Depending on the situation, for example if I was talking to a sales manager, then I may have told a slightly more detailed version of this story. I may have also shared more details if they were fascinated by my short story and said something like, "Really, how did you achieve that?" I never had it scripted, but my longer version of the story would have been something like the example below.

Long Story Example:

01 **Framing up the problem:**
I was working for a company that sold HR Software solutions. The company had appointment setters, and as a software sales rep I would walk into the office with a completely full calendar every day. My job was to demo HR software to sell software subscriptions. It was fast paced, and I would do 12 to 15 demos per day. It was normal to follow up with a customer in order to close the sale. One day I realized that I had a great conversation on a prior demo call but never followed up. Somehow, I had completely forgotten the person's name and for some reason couldn't find it in my notes. I knew this meeting had occurred but with no name or company name to search for, I didn't know how to find the record in Salesforce.

02 **What did I do about it:**
I ended up creating a simple report that showed all of my opportunities in an open status; with a probability and a dollar value assigned but no future scheduled activity (no future task or events). I ran the report and immediately found the customer I was trying to remember, plus several more records that had fallen through the cracks that I didn't even know about. I knew I was deeply engaged within my role, so I thought if this if this is happening with me, then it's happening with others. I updated the report and ran it for the whole company and discovered about $17mil a year in potential revenue was just never being followed up on. I ended up making a few variations of the report and creating a dashboard. After sharing my findings with the sales leadership team, we made the dashboard available to all the Sales Reps.

03 **Benefits:**
We found that about 20% of those opportunities were closable, and over the next year the company saw over $3mil in additional sales.

If you are just starting off and you have never even worked in a job that required you to use Salesforce as an end user, then your story may be related to your training and leveraging your knowledge of the Salesforce platform. For example, you may be asked a question where you respond: "That reminds me of a trailhead exercise I did recently where a company is faced with the problem of _____, and I built out a solution by doing _____, and it solved the problem."

Activity begets activity. It may seem like a lot but over time you will trade up for better stories to tell. You will undoubtedly implement some solution and feel the satisfaction that comes from solving a real-world problem. If the thought of: "Hey, this would be a good story to tell" ever crosses your mind, then remember to write it down or shoot yourself an email. These stories will serve as a great resource for you in the future to be able to quickly prepare for an interview if the need should ever arise.

6.11. Remember that interviews go both ways.

The best way to succeed in a Salesforce.com Administrator role is by selecting the right job to begin with. Remember that job interviews are just as much about you learning about the company as it is about them learning about you. During your interview process, be sure to ask questions that center around the scope of work and responsibility of the position and any additional training or certification support offered by the company to help you hone your Salesforce.com skills.

6.12. Don't over commit.

Be honest about your abilities. Never lie about your skillset or experience level. It's good to be stretched, but overselling yourself will only come back to bite you. Remember, it's not just about getting the job but also about doing the job once you get it. If you get into a company and truly add value to the organization, then you will gain highly valuable experiences that will give you a foundation to build your career.

However, the opposite can be true as well. If you "land a job" but you are consistently underperforming due to your personal skill level not being adequate to meet the needs of the particular role, then this can create a dark energy around you and set you back in your career progress. Being stretched can lead to accelerated growth, but being overly stretched can cause you to break.

Some jobs include technical requirements that start to cross over the line from Salesforce Administrator to Salesforce Developer. Be clear on which parts of the platform require code, and don't be afraid to speak up if that's beyond your current skillset. Salesforce prides itself in being a no code/low code platform. You can still be very confident about your abilities and the solutions you can deliver on the declarative side of the platform.

6.13. Adapting Your Interview Preparation for the Virtual Setting

As remote work becomes more common, virtual interviews are becoming increasingly popular. To ensure your success in this setting, consider the following tips when preparing for a virtual Salesforce Administrator interview:

1. **Test your technology:**
    Ensure your computer, webcam, and microphone are functioning correctly before the interview. Test your internet connection for stability, and make sure you have a reliable video conferencing platform installed. Familiarize yourself with the platform's features, such as screen sharing, in case you need to demonstrate your Salesforce skills.

2. **Choose an appropriate setting:**
    Select a quiet, well-lit, and clutter-free location for your interview. Make sure your background is professional and free of distractions. Position your camera at eye level to maintain good eye contact with the interviewer.

3. **Dress professionally:**
    Just like in an in-person interview, dress appropriately for the role and company culture. Even though the interview is virtual, maintaining a professional appearance demonstrates your commitment to the opportunity.

4. **Practice non-verbal communication:**

In a virtual interview, non-verbal cues are crucial. Maintain eye contact, sit up straight, and use hand gestures to emphasize points when appropriate. Be mindful of your facial expressions and avoid fidgeting.

5. **Prepare for technical challenges:**

Have a backup plan in case you experience technical difficulties during the interview. This might include having an alternative device or video conferencing platform ready, or a phone number to call the interviewer if needed.

6. **Adapt your storytelling:**

When sharing your Salesforce experiences, ensure you can effectively communicate your stories through the virtual setting. Be prepared to share your screen if necessary to demonstrate specific examples or showcase your work.

7. **Engage with the interviewer:**

In a virtual interview, it's essential to be proactive in engaging with the interviewer. Ask questions, show enthusiasm, and listen attentively. Make sure your body language conveys your interest and professionalism.

8. **Send a follow-up email:**

After the interview, send a thank-you email to the interviewer, expressing your appreciation for their time and reiterating your interest in the role. This gesture helps you stand out and demonstrates your commitment to the opportunity.

By adapting your interview preparation for the virtual setting, you can increase your chances of success and show your adaptability as a Salesforce Administrator in today's evolving work environment.

Preparing For an Interview Conclusion

While you may not ace your first interview or secure the first job you apply for, remember that practice makes perfect. By diligently following the strategies and suggestions outlined in this chapter, you can accelerate your learning curve and significantly enhance your chances of interview success. Stay committed to refining your interviewing skills, and remain confident in your abilities as a Salesforce Administrator to create a lasting impression on potential employers.

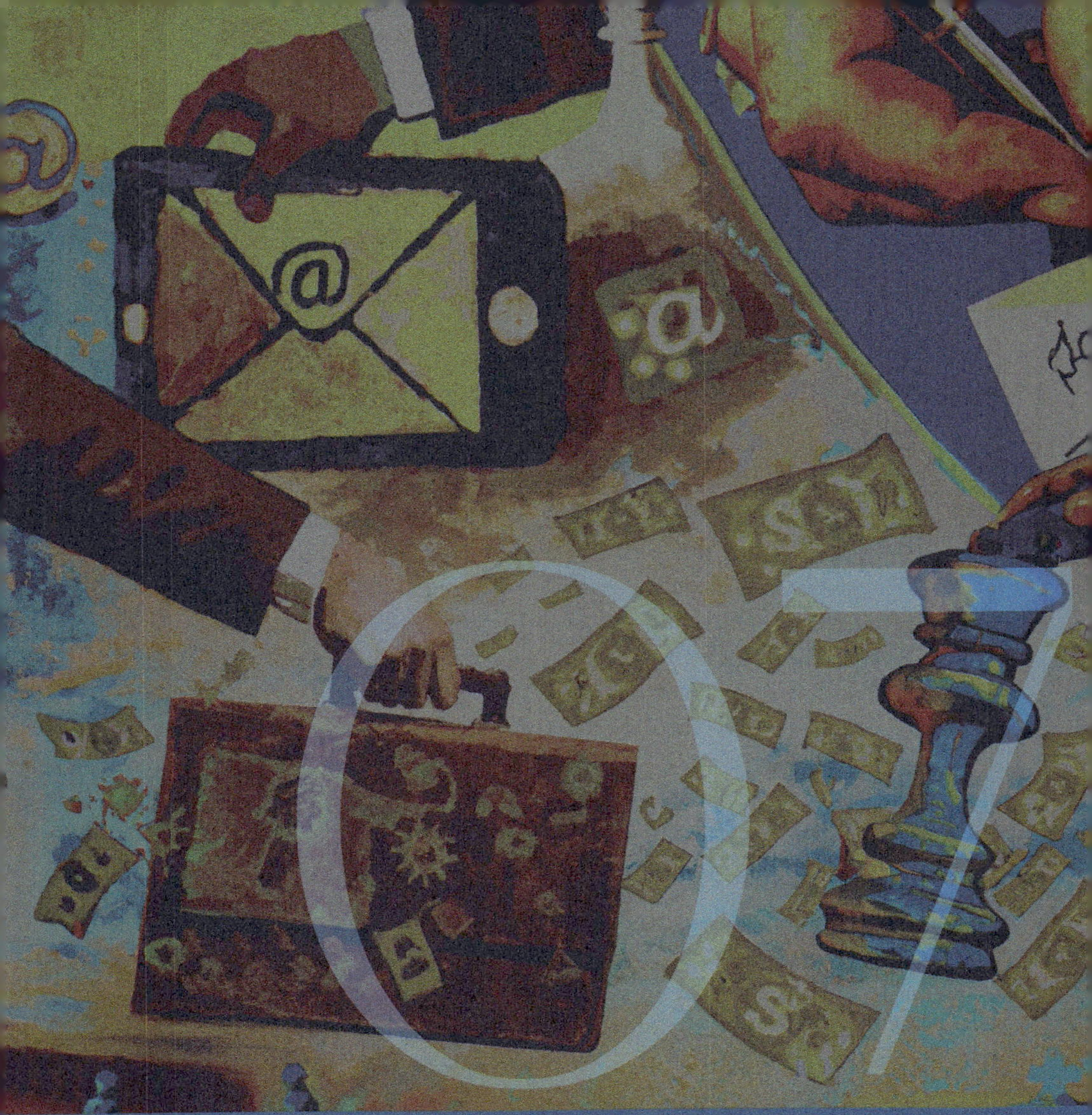

07

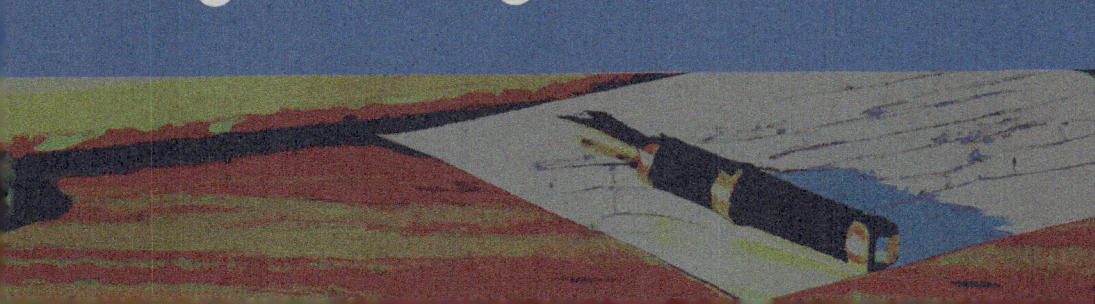

Considerations for Negotiating Salaries

7.1.   When To Negotiate

There are two primary reasons to negotiate a salary:

1.   The offer you received is obviously lacking when compared to what your skill level, experience level, and other qualifications are valued at in the open market. This is the main reason you would ever attempt to negotiate.

2.   You are new to a Salesforce career, and you sincerely cannot meet the needs of you and your family based on the offer received, but it's a very marginal difference. This may be the case for example if you are coming from a non-Salesforce role and doing a career pivot into Salesforce. Let's say you are accustomed to making a certain amount per year but you receive an offer as a junior administrator with a salary that's 10% lower than your current non-Salesforce position. It would be understandable if you were to attempt to negotiate with the reasoning that although you are excited to pivot into the position, you cannot afford a cut in pay.

7.1.1.   Why Might You Consider Taking a Pay Cut When Pivoting Into a Salesforce Career?

Although most all career moves are done with the goal of seeking a better circumstance (including pay), sometimes you may need to take a couple steppingstones to help you reach your ultimate goal. If you are currently working in a non-Salesforce role and you are looking to do a career pivot into a Salesforce position, then depending on all the variables within your individual circumstance, it may make sense to take a position with lateral pay or even a slight decrease in pay. You're probably asking yourself why this may be a strategy to consider? Let's review a few things to see why this could even be a consideration.

7.1.2.   First, Let's Take a Look at the Salesforce Salary Averages:

According to ZipRecruiter.com, as of December 18th 2022 the average annual pay for a Salesforce Administrator in the United States is $90,048 a year.

The same salary report states: "While ZipRecruiter is seeing annual salaries as high as $143,500 and as low as $39,000, the majority of Salesforce Administrator salaries currently range between $69,000 (25th percentile) to $107,000 (75th percentile) with top earners (90th percentile) making $127,000 annually across the United States. The average pay range for a Salesforce Administrator varies greatly (by as much as $38,000), which suggests there may be many opportunities for advancement and increased pay based on skill level, location, and years of experience."

7.1.3.   An Opportunity & Challenge

Obviously, the individual Salesforce.com Administrators who are earning the top end of the pay range are typically those with the most experience and skills to offer. This presents both an opportunity and a challenge: all you have to do to increase your earnings to a respectable $90k a year (average Salesforce Administrator earnings) is gain some experience and sharpen your skills to at least the "average" level; but how do you gain experience or skills without a Salesforce job that allows you to learn something new every day by working on the platform to solve real life business problems? This can be a bit of a paradox, but many have chosen to overcome this by making short-term compromises in exchange for mid- to long-term rewards.

Example Scenario

For example: if you make $50k a year in your non-Salesforce related role, and you are offered a job that pays $45k as a Junior Admin, you have three options:

OPTION 01	Attempt to negotiate to at least keep your salary the same as your current position. This may or may not be successful considering your lack of experience.
OPTION 02	Hold out for a better opportunity. This option may or may not work out considering opportunities are fewer with limited experience and skills.
OPTION 03	Agree to take the position for slightly lesser pay knowing that in 12 to 24 months you will have added a considerable amount of experience and gained some success stories to tell. In addition, during this time you'll probably pick up an additional certification or two, and you realize that you will be able to transfer these skills and experience to a Salesforce Administrator role (not "Junior Level") for a considerable pay bump. This transfer may be either within the same company or organization or a new job at a different company all together.

Which Option do You Choose?

There is no one right answer as to which of these three options to choose. Everyone's situation is different, with much variation and uniqueness in their past experiences, technical skill levels, and natural soft skills. There is no one size fits all approach that will work across the board. However, if you have the understanding that there is a significant level of opportunity available to those who find enjoyment in helping solve business problems on the Salesforce.com platform, then this awareness may help guide some of your decision making.

Going back to our example: if you are accustomed to making $50k a year but you know that the odds are extremely high that you could be earning $70k to $90k in just 18 to 24 months (and perhaps $127k within just a few years), then this could be enough to persuade you to be willing to take a $5k reduction in pay for that first year or two.

I do find it rather surprising that it's completely acceptable within our society for people to attend a four-year university while incurring tens of thousands of dollars in debt each year, and earning zero income during this time, and come out with a degree that offers no certainty of a job. Yet these same people are often times so shortsighted after entering their career that they are unwilling to take a little pay cut for junior admin role when it has a nearly 100% chance of doubling or even tripling their income over a four-year period.

According to the Bureau of Labor Statistics, the median annual wage across all occupations within the United States as of May 2021 is $45,760. Consider that even the most entry level Salesforce Junior Admin position will probably be at this number (or perhaps even better), and you will have a runway to double or even triple your salary within just a few short years. No University degree required. No student loans required. No computer coding skills required. How many industries do you know of that consistently allow individuals with no college degree to have the same outcome?

Considerations for Negotiating Salaries

7.1.4.   Salary Negotiation Considerations

Negotiating a salary and benefits package for a Salesforce Administrator job can be intimidating, but it's important to remember that you have value and worth as an employee. That said, you also want to be realistic in balancing your expectations with your experience level. If you decide that you need to negotiate, here are some steps you can take to negotiate a fair and rewarding package:

01   **Research the market:**
Find out what other Salesforce Administrators with your same experience level in your area are earning. Look at salary surveys, job postings, and networking with other professionals in the field. This will give you a good idea of what to expect and what you should aim for in terms of salary.

02   **Know your worth:**
Consider your skills and experience when determining your salary expectations. Be realistic, but don't sell yourself short.

03   **Make a list of your priorities:**
Decide what is most important to you in terms of benefits and salary. For example, you may prioritize a higher salary over additional vacation days, or vice versa, or perhaps having the flexibility of working in a remote (work from home) position is worth more to you than a higher salary.

04   **Practice your negotiation skills:**
Role-play with a friend or mentor to help you feel more prepared and confident during the negotiation process.

05   **Communicate your value:**
When negotiating, be sure to highlight your skills, experience, and achievements that make you a valuable candidate for the position.

06   **Be open to compromise:**
Remember that salary and benefits negotiations are a two-way street. You may not get everything you want, but try to find a middle ground that works for both you and the employer. Negotiate in a professional way. Don't give an ultimatum or draw hard lines.

07 **Don't be afraid to negotiate but do it with the right attitude:**

It's important to remember that it's okay to advocate for yourself and negotiate for a fair salary and benefits package. Look for what is fair to you and fair to the company. Don't be afraid to speak up and negotiate, as long as you do it professionally and respectfully and your request is reasonable/fair.

7.1.5.   Be Humble. Be Grateful. Be Considerate:

If you chose to negotiate, be sure to humbly and respectfully present your case with logic and reason. You don't want to come across as entitled or arrogant. Start and end the conversation with gratitude. Thank them for the opportunity with gratefulness and

excitement. Present your case respectfully while being honest about your reasoning for why you need a higher salary. Part of being professional is giving them a way out, thanking them for their consideration while making them feel like they can safely deliver bad news (like sorry this is the best we can do) if it comes to that.

Salary negotiations can be a delicate thing. If everyone agrees that you are a good fit for the position, and you are truly excited and full of appreciation, then it naturally causes the hiring manager to want to be an advocate for you. If they really like you and you're being reasonable in your requests, then they will most likely go to bat for you and try to help you. If you come across as an entitled arrogant millennial, you can easily rub them the wrong way. If they stop liking you, then they certainly aren't going to want to help you.

Try to put yourself in their shoes and imagine all the pressure they must be under to get someone hired into the role. Also imagine how difficult it may be for them to have to operate within whatever salary ranges have been allocated during their annual budget planning for their business. Consider that they are short staffed until the position is filled, and this hiring manager may be facing additional pressure daily due to being shorthanded. Be sensitive to the fact that the hiring manager is a person also. Just like you have stress placed on you by having to go through the hiring process, the hiring manager is probably hit with additional stressors as well.

7.1.6.   Don't Be Memorable for the Wrong Reasons:

I once had a position open for a Salesforce.com Administrator. At that time, we didn't have a tremendously large pool of candidates to choose from. I met with someone who was recently certified and had no Salesforce experience. She seemed to carry herself well in a very professional manner. I knew that she was extremely new in her career and would need lots of input, but I could tell that she was smart and had the potential to do a good job in the role. At my company there were rumors rapidly circulating about an upcoming hiring freeze. I was in a situation that if I didn't make someone an offer, then I likely would lose the ability to hire anyone at all. My boss and I agreed that she had great potential and so we decided to offer her the job.

At some point during the interview process, she had shared how much she was making in her current job. We offered her a position that would have come with a new base salary that was about 15% higher than her current role's total compensation; plus the new position came with a 10% annual incentive pay that gave the opportunity to make even more. I knew that this person had zero experience, but I was willing to take a chance because I believed that she was a quick learner with lots of potential; and I knew that there would soon be a companywide hiring freeze and any open positions would be frozen.

I called her with the good news and was truly excited to extend to her the opportunity. I quickly learned that this person was educated enough to know what Salesforce.com jobs could pay, but she didn't give any consideration at all to her lack of experience. She very matter of factly insisted that she be paid more. I reminded her that this was already a significant pay bump, informed her of the many other generous parts of the overall benefits package, and explained to her that she would have the opportunity to earn more in a very short time by getting some experience and obtaining an additional certification (which the company was willing to pay for). She coldly responded: "Nope, I have to have $X amount." There was no explanation. No logic involved. No reasoning. No gratitude. No consideration. No humility. Up until this point, she had been an absolute pleasure, and I was admittedly a bit taken back by her chosen strategy for negotiation. After some quick internal discussions, we ended up countering her counteroffer and settling on a number somewhere in between. In time, she became a good resource, and eventually moved on to something better. We had a great working relationship, and even now I wish her all the best, but I never forgot the shock from the coarseness and arrogance in the chosen salary negotiation response.

Never negotiate simply for the sake of "more." Sure, everybody may want to earn more money, but that alone should not be a reason for negotiating. All negotiations should be market-based or need-based. If your negotiation request is presented as more money for the sake of more money, then it will likely not go well for you.

Negotiation Conclusion

To recap: Consider if a lateral pay move or even taking a job for slightly lesser pay would be a good mid-term strategy for you. Remember to be realistic about where your skill and experience level is within the market. Find what is fair to the company and fair to you. If you find yourself in a scenario where you need to negotiate, then don't be afraid to negotiate, but do it with the right attitude. Be humble. Be grateful. Be considerate. Don't be memorable for the wrong reasons. Don't seek "more for the sake of more." Support your request with market-based data.

Salesforce Jedi Wisdom

We've discussed how a Salesforce Administrator role is a blend of both technical and soft skills. We'll now look at some basic tips on how to succeed as a Salesforce.com Administrator so you can start your journey in the right direction. This chapter is about adopting a general mentally; changing the way you think in any given situation. These are general principals to live by and are listed in no particular order. I do hope the principles conveyed here will serve you well for many years to come and help guide your day-to-day decision making.

8.1.　Be Proactive

Take ownership in the role and strive to learn as much as possible about all aspects of Salesforce.com as well as the business you serve. Seek out additional training opportunities that will enhance your knowledge and skill set. Offer up ideas for improvement or new processes that can help streamline or improve workflow.

8.2.　Communicate Effectively

Good communication is essential for any job, but it's especially important in a Salesforce Administrator role. Develop your skills by actively engaging with all stakeholders and making sure that everyone understands the objective of projects. Make sure to clearly explain complex technical concepts to non-technical coworkers. I've found that visual process flows can be of great value.

8.3.　Continually Improve

The Salesforce.com platform is constantly changing, so it's important to stay ahead of the curve by regularly reading blogs and articles related to the platform and exploring new features or options within Salesforce. This will help you understand how things have changed over time as well as any potential problems that may arise in the future.

8.4.　Focus on Quality

Always focus on quality over quantity when it comes to your work. Make sure that all changes and updates are thoroughly tested and debugged before going live. Quality will be key for creating a successful user experience, so take the time needed to ensure everything is working correctly and as expected.

8.5. Functioning as Designed vs. Functioning as Desired

Functioning as designed refers to the system operating in accordance with its intended design. It means the product is working as intended and meeting the business requirements that was originally specified. Functioning as desired, on the other hand, refers to the product operating in a way that satisfies the user's needs and expectations. It means the product not only meets its design specifications but also satisfies the user's requirements and preferences in terms of performance, usability, and overall satisfaction. In other words, functioning as designed refers to the technical aspects of a product, while functioning as desired refers to the user's experience and satisfaction with the product.

8.6. What problem are we trying to solve?

Remember this question. Ask it daily. This is your one job... too often, discussions start with proposed solutions. Assumptions are made, and solutions are half-baked. Make sure you understand for every stakeholder's perspective the problem at hand that needs to be solved.

8.7. Don't Let Great Get in the Way of Good Enough

Okay, so this one will no doubt raise a few eyebrows, but don't let great get in the way of good enough. If you can solve 80% of a problem now and the remaining 20% incrementally over the course of the next weeks, months, or even years; then do it! Far too often companies try to solve everything at once and delay any progress at all until everything can be solved in one shot. This can especially be true at larger organizations. Generally speaking, if you wait until you can solve for everything, then you'll solve nothing. Ask yourself and your team: **"How can we do the most good now?"** I'm not suggesting that everything becomes the wild west where you shot from the hip and ask questions later. You do need to be well-informed, know as much about the problems as you can, and understand any potential ripple effects of your planned solution. However, in most cases, agile incremental improvements beat out old school waterfall methodologies almost every time.

8.8.   Fail Fast and Move Forward

Too often people get stuck in analysis paralysis, and the fear of making the wrong decision keeps them from making any decision at all. Make educated decisions based on the input from all stakeholders. Test planned changes in a sandbox with all needed UAT and validations prior to deploying. Demo solutions for the stakeholders, and if all agree, then proceed to deployment. Monitor results, share outcomes, and adjust as needed.

8.9.   It's Okay to Loose, Just Don't Loose Alone

We of course never want to put ourselves or our companies in a scenario where we aren't winning, but in the Salesforce world there is a direct correlation between the requirements you gather and the success of the solutions you design. It's best not to go rogue when attempting to solve a problem. Include others in the discussion to ensure that you have a full understanding of the challenges and that everyone agrees on the solution.

8.10. Proverbs 18 - One Man Seems Right Until Another Man Speaks

When learning about a problem, it's best to get multiple perspectives. Sometimes really smart people are still wrong. It can be easy to trust the opinion of one person, or worse; to feel obligated based on the person's position or authoritative demeanor, but when requirements gathering, it would be prudent to get more than one opinion.

8.11. Create Visuals When Getting Agreement

Learn to use Microsoft Visio or similar tools if you find yourself frequently discussing multi-step business processes. Sometimes two people think they are saying the same thing and it's not until they see it that they realize that there's some nuance that makes it different. If mapping out processes in a swim lane style chart, then be sure to include what happens, in which system, by whom, and in what process step order.

8.12.   Find a Mentor and Network

One of the best ways to learn how to become a successful Salesforce Administrator is by finding someone in the industry who can mentor you. Not only can they provide invaluable advice and guidance, but having a mentor will also give you the opportunity to network with other professionals in the industry. These connections are key to advancing your career as well as staying up to date on new trends and technologies.

8.13.   Make Learning Fun!

It's important to have fun while you learn, so don't forget to take breaks and try something new. Whether it's taking a coding class, attending a webinar, or just reading up on the Salesforce platform—make sure you're enjoying yourself! All of these activities can provide insight into best practices and tips for becoming an expert in the Salesforce world.

8.14.   Know Who to Ask

Meet people within your organization. Understand the value each person brings and know which pieces of the process they touch. You may need to loop them into various discussions for additional perspectives on problems or potential process changes.

8.15.   Prioritize User Experience

Always put the user experience first when trying to solve a problem. This can be an arduous process, but it's well worth it in the end. The simpler and easier your solution is to use, the better off you'll be in terms of user adoption rate. Striving for simplicity should always be top of mind.

8.16.   Monitor Solution Performance

When making changes, it's important to measure their effectiveness. Make sure you have a baseline before starting, and then track the success of your efforts so that you can prove your work is having an effect. This will also help you continue to make improvements down the road. You go through a lot of effort to fully understand a problem; then you make process changes within as "counter measures" to resolve the issue, but you oftentimes need to monitor the ongoing performance of the solution you implemented. This will help ensure that the issue doesn't reoccur. Your "monitoring" may be as simple as a Salesforce report that automatically alerts when conditions are met in order to make you aware of any records where a problem reoccurred.

8.17. Celebrate Your Successes

Don't forget to celebrate when you make a major breakthrough. It can be easy to focus on the negative aspects of working to correct process issues and forget about all the successes along the way, but it's important to recognize when achievements and milestones are made. Celebrating will also help you and your stakeholders stay motivated and keep pushing forward. While change management can bring positive outcomes and benefits, it can also be a difficult and challenging process as it often involves disrupting established systems, processes, and ways of working. Employees may resist change, and the transition can be stressful and painful, especially for those who are attached to the current way of doing things. **By communicating successes out to your users, stakeholders and up to your leadership, over time you will develop a track record of success and it will become easier to get buy-in for making additional changes that are needed within the system.**

8.18. Manage Up

Managing up is a critical skill for anyone looking to advance their career, and it involves setting expectations with your management in an effective and positive way. Here are some helpful tips on how to manage up:

1. Have a clear understanding of your objectives and communicate them effectively.

2. Ask questions and build a relationship with your supervisor.

3. Be proactive in proposing ideas for improvement or change.

4. Provide candid feedback about areas requiring attention.

5. Take ownership of tasks and responsibilities assigned to you by management.

6. Be positive, flexible, reliable, and respectful at all times.

7. Ensure expectations are realistic, achievable, and mutually beneficial for both parties involved.

8.19. Leaders Lead

You don't need to be assigned an official leadership role in order to demonstrate the characteristics and qualities of a good leader. There are no shortage of problems within any business. Many of these problems are just waiting for someone to take the initiative to solve them. If you see something, say something. Surface issues as you can, even if you know you can't fully address them right away. Add them to backlog, get agreement on solutions, and work through them like you would any other issue that is raised within the business.

I'm certain that there are a number of principals that could be added to this section, and these listed so far have only begun to scratch the surface. However, I do hope that these few tips help you succeed as a Salesforce.com Administrator. Remember that success is not an overnight process but rather something that takes time and dedication. Be patient, stay motivated, and never stop learning!

09

Software Development Lifecycle

The Software Development Lifecycle is a process that covers the development of a software system from its conception to its eventual retirement. This process involves various stages which include planning, analysis, design, implementation, testing, and maintenance. Each stage builds on the previous one and culminates in the successful delivery of a functional product or system.

There were certainly times early in my career when I sat in a conference room full of IT people and felt a little intimidated by all their knowledge of processes and use of various buzzwords that I didn't seem to understand. I would take notes of random terminology that they were using throughout our meetings, and although I could generally follow along with the overall context of the meeting, it wasn't until I would get back to my desk and commence Googling that I would become fully up to speed.

The goal of this chapter is to give you a high-level understanding of all the various steps that are commonly involved in the management of a Salesforce environment.

Note that there is not one single "correct way" of managing software deployments on Salesforce. Each company's process steps may vary based on the complexity and size of their Salesforce Org, as well as the level of regulatory oversight within their industry. I've assisted a number of companies with designing and developing Salesforce solutions, and I've seen some companies on both ends of the spectrum. Some with extremely overly regulated, arduous processes, other companies who seem to have no process at all, and then some that are somewhere in the middle.

The company you ultimately go to work for will have their own procedures for how they choose to manage Salesforce deployments, and you will no doubt learn a lot about the Software Development Lifecycle with each company that you have the opportunity to serve. My hope is that this chapter will give you enough of a general understanding that you won't be lost if someone wants to talk about software deployment best practices, or if the topic should come up during a job interview.

9.1.   11 Steps in The Software Development Lifecycle

As previously stated, the steps involved in overall management of changes within a Salesforce Org may vary based on the company's specific procedures. That said, you're not guaranteed to see all of these process steps within every company, and some companies may even have additional steps within their processes that we are not covering here. However, the following 11 steps should give you a pretty good idea of system changes that can be managed within most companies.

We will first list out all 11 steps, and then we will discuss each individual step within this chapter.

In the following pages we will take a deeper look at what is involved within each of these steps.

9.1.1.   STEP 1: Operate & Maintain the System

The process begins with operating and maintaining the system. This includes:

- ✦ Managing user accounts
- ✦ Assisting with password resets
- ✦ Data management activities
- ✦ Managing reports and dashboards
- ✦ Responding to any general support request
- ✦ And basically all other maintenance related activity that is required to keep things up and going.

Who's Involved?

Most of these activities will fall on the Salesforce Administrator.

9.1.2.   STEP 2: Collect Business/User Feedback & Create Future Requirements

As daily management processes are carried out, you collect feedback from the business and the end users that often result in the creation of new future requirements by listening to the end users and the key stakeholders. You can learn what works well and what doesn't work in the system.

This feedback helps you to understand what problems you need to solve, which results in the creation of additional requirements for the system.

Who's Involved?

Many of these activities could be led by Salesforce Administrator, Developer, Business Analyst, Architect, Product Owner, or others. However, collecting feedback from the business and users of a Salesforce org typically involves stakeholders from different departments including sales teams, customer service teams, IT professionals, and executives.

9.1.3.   STEP 3: Analyze User Requirements

Once the requirements are outlined, you're probably going to end up in a deep dive session where you analyze the user requirements and write user stories by whiteboarding the additional planning details for each individual requirement.

You're going to gain a clearer understanding of the requirement and how it fits into the larger workflow process. This basically gives you a better understanding of exactly what problem you're trying to solve.

Who's Involved?

Analyzing user requirements for a Salesforce project typically involves stakeholders from different departments as well as Product Owners, Admins, Developers, IT professionals, Business Analysts, and Quality Assurance Specialists. These stakeholders must collaborate to ensure that the results accurately reflect the needs of the users. Often, this is not a single event but done as a series of meetings which may start with a smaller core team grow into a larger group as additional buy-in is required.

9.1.4.   STEP 4: Design the Solution

After the requirements are gathered, it's in the design phase of the process that you determine which direction to go for a solution. It's in this step that you'll identify the technical features or components to be used for the planned solution.

The design phase will take into account things like the rules for how the business should run, the things it needs to keep track of, and what information is needed for each of those things. It will also look at things like how tasks should be done automatically, how tasks should be approved, and what rules need to be followed to make sure things are done correctly. This phase will also look at the bigger picture and decide if programming is needed to make the solution work. Note that with Salesforce.com, it's generally considered the best practice to use the declarative Salesforce features before jumping to a custom coded solution.

Who's Involved?

Much of these tasks fall onto Salesforce Architects & Developers, but if you work as an Admin for a company that doesn't have these resources, then you may find yourself doing solution design also.

9.1.5.   STEP 5: Implement the Solution

And now for the fun part of the project, the implementation phase, this is where you begin to put all the pieces together; you create the needed data structure by adding files to standard or custom objects.

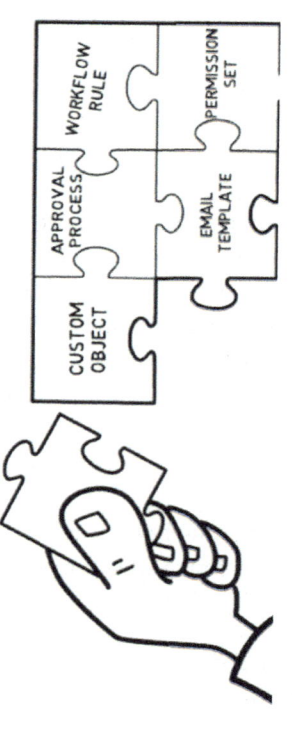

You create any required workflow by using Flows, the Process Builder, or code. If required, you add in the approval processes or validation rules and you double check your Org Wide Default (OWD) sharing settings and profile permissions for each of the items included in the release. This is where you begin to see the idea come to life.

Who's Involved?

Much like designing the solution, much of the implementation of the solution will vary based on the size of the company that you work for, as well as the procedures the company has in place for managing system changes. Typically, the Salesforce.com Administrators and Developers will be responsible for all configuration changes that are required to implement the solution within the Salesforce sandbox environment.

9.1.6.   STEP 6: Pre-release QA

Once you've completed constructing the desired features in the sandbox, it's time for the prerelease quality assurance testing in this step of the process. A group of testers will test the new functionality and provide feedback.

This initial round of testing is often completed by developers or administrators, but it may also include the same users or key stakeholders who requested the new features.

This validation step ensures that no key elements of the solution are missing from the design. Note that if you're consistently find changes being requested in this step, it could be a sign that there's not enough details being gathered when writing requirements and user stories.

Who's Involved?

Pre-Release QA Testing in a Salesforce sandbox environment typically involves stakeholders from different departments, including Product Owners, Salesforce Administrators, Developers, IT professionals, Business Analysts, and Quality Assurance Specialists.

9.1.7.   STEP 7: Documentation

Let's take a minute to discuss some technical documentation needs before you can progress to the user acceptance testing phase; you need to have some test scripts for the U.A.T. testers to follow.

These scripts are ideally written by technical writers who receive input from developers or Salesforce administrators, but oftentimes the Salesforce Administrator may be responsible for helping to write these test instructions if there is no Technical Writer on the team.

In addition to the test script, you may also need to create some release notes to help communicate the changes to the users and some technical documentation to help yourself and others understand how the solution was built.

Documentation can also include information about bug fixes, new features, updates, or changes that have been made to the software. Furthermore, it can help new users understand how to use the software and quickly find answers to common questions they may have.

> **DOCUMENTATION SIDENOTE:**
> As a helpful side note, it's always a good idea to ensure that the technical solution is well documented, since in the future you may be asked to modify the items in this release, or you may be asked to build something new but similar in functionality.

There are two key takeaways when it comes to technical documentation:

✦ The first is, generally speaking, six months from now, you're probably not going to remember what you did today.

✦ And when you're trying to remember or understand how something was built, it's typically easier to reference a technical document versus being forced to reverse engineer it.

Who's Involved?

Documentation is typically created by Admins, Developers, Business Analysts and Technical Writers.

9.1.8.   STEP 8: UAT Testing

User acceptance testing allows for a select group of end users who are experts at their business processes to take the test scripts produced in the documentation phase and execute each test step that was included in the script. They would then sign off on each test script stating whether the results of their testing matched the expected results described on the script. In some cases, users may be required to provide screenshots as objective evidence to prove that the test passed.

Some industries, such as health care and finance, have more government and regulatory oversight. If you're managing the Salesforce.com environment in one of these industries, then you may be required to follow a more stringent documentation process of your testing activities.

Who's Involved?

UAT Test Scripts are typically executed by Quality Assurance Specialists or some selected end users from within the Salesforce Org.

9.1.9.   STEP 9: Ensure Compliance

Individual companies may also choose to add some compliance steps to their process, but these additional steps will vary from company to company, depending on many different factors, including the:

Industry & regulatory oversight – some industries such as Finance or Healthcare have more stringent requirements for how data is handled and may be regulators to oversee how you operate, including the ability for different agencies to perform audits to ensure compliance.

Type of data being stored in the Salesforce.com environment.
Personal Information is things used to identify someone such as their name, email, and phone number.
Sensitive Information is a type of personal information that is more highly protected by laws due to its more vulnerable nature (SSN, religion, political affiliation, criminal history, credit report, etc.).

Who's Involved?

Compliance is everyone's job. Each person is expected to consider compliance requirements at every step in the process.

9.1.10.   STEP 10: User Training

You will need to consider if any training is required before moving your changes to production, in some cases the changes may not require any training, such as new backend workflow processes that perform calculations or automates email communications.

In other cases, when changes are user-facing, then you will need to consider how to best educate the users on the changes.

TRAINING FORMATS:

 **Email:** Training your users could be as simple as an email informing the users of the changes, including a screenshot which displays the change.

 **Video:** It could be a pre-recorded video that demonstrates the new features.

 **Virtual Live Demo:** You may offer a web session where you share a live demo and to take questions.

 **In Person Meeting:** And, of course, you could even have a good old fashion in person meeting in a conference room to review what's new within your Salesforce Org.

The type of training that you provide will most likely depend on the scope and size of the changes to your user's experience.

Simply put, large changes require more change management.

Who's Involved?

Training Content Development: Generally, the creation of user training may be the responsibility of the Salesforce administrator, Salesforce developer, technical writer, or online learning designer. They will collaborate with any stakeholders to ensure that all content is accurate and meets the needs of the intended audience.

Training Delivery: After the training content is produced, there are different roles that may bear the responsibility of delivering the training to the end users. It's quite common for the Salesforce administrator to be engaged with the end users within their Salesforce Org, including the delivery of training on new features. In some companies there may be additional resources tasked with delivering the training such as: a dedicated Salesforce.com trainer, customer service representatives, technical support staff, or other key stakeholder (such as a manager training the members of their own team).

9.1.11. STEP 11: Production Deployment

Finally, you're ready to move your changes to production with Salesforce. This is typically achieved by packaging up all the individual components created in the development process into a "Change Set," and pushing that Change Set from the sandbox to the production world where it would be validated and deployed. **Note that it is also a good practice to perform some post deployment regression testing to ensure that nothing went wrong with the release.**

In addition, another best practice is using the developer sandbox for your build and having your initial deployment go from the developer sandbox to the full copy sandbox for testing. This allows developers to practice their deployments and learn in advance if they should expect any challenges when moving the items to production.

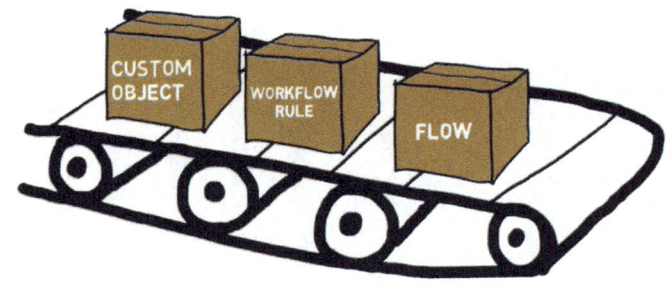

Who's Involved?

Deployments could be managed by Salesforce administrators and/or developers; both are fairly common. Larger companies may have more complex deployment strategies which involve more people.

11 Steps Conclusion and Disclaimers

This concludes the 11 steps that are often found in the software development lifecycle on the Salesforce.com platform.

Note that the circle is directionally correct. However, this circle depicts all of these steps in a somewhat linear fashion.

In reality, each individual business or organization may have a process that varies slightly, but if you are establishing a new set of procedures for an organization, you should at least consider each of these 11 steps.

It's important to note that this process can involve many different individuals, and that everyone's role may have ownership of different steps within the process. Furthermore, these individuals may sometimes perform their steps of the process in parallel to one another.

For example: a compliance officer or a Q&R (Quality & Regulatory) representative may be heavily consulted by a business analyst, architect, or developer as they are analyzing the user requirements, designing and implementing the solution. So, ensuring compliance is not a single step within the process but is considered throughout.

Another important note is the order in which the steps are performed may also slightly vary. For example, user training for a specific new feature may not actually occur until after the production release.

How to Gather Project Requirements

10.1. Introduction to Project Requirements Gathering

In this section we will discuss how to gather requirements for a Salesforce.com project, and different questions to consider when making changes to Salesforce.com.

When you're gathering requirements for any Salesforce.com project, this is not a task to be taken lightly. There are several critical questions that need to be answered before any design or development work can take place. Sometimes if you're new to Salesforce project management, or new to requirements gathering in general, it can be easy to get overwhelmed. The purpose of this chapter is to provide some simple guidance on things to do and questions to ask when gathering requirements for changes to be made in Salesforce. By the end of this chapter, you will be able to adopt a simple project management template that will help you:

✦ Facilitate meaningful discussions within your workplace.

✦ Ensure all the correct stakeholders are engaged in your project.

✦ Help guide productive dialogues to determine the most important problems to be solved for your organization.

✦ Get agreement from all key stakeholders on which potential solutions would best meet the needs of the business and when they need to be delivered.

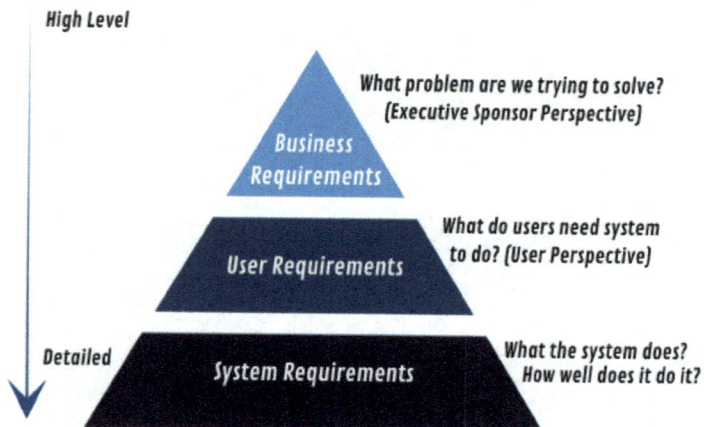

10.2.   Six Things to Consider When Planning a Salesforce Project

Here are six things to consider when planning a Salesforce.com project.

Goals:
What are the goals and objectives of this project?

Stakeholders:
Who is involved in the project?

Key Deliverables:
What are the key deliverables for the project?

Success Metric:
How will you measure success for this project?

Deadlines:
When do you need to have this project completed by?

Priority Level:
What's the priority level for each requested change?

At the most basic level, just asking these questions may give you a pretty good idea as to what changes to create within the system and how to deliver these changes. However, let's take this a step further and look at these same six topics in the following sections within this chapter and consider other questions that you may want to ask to ensure you gather an adequate level of details to help everyone recognize the various nuances involved in the problems you are trying to solve, as well as agreement on the best potential solutions.

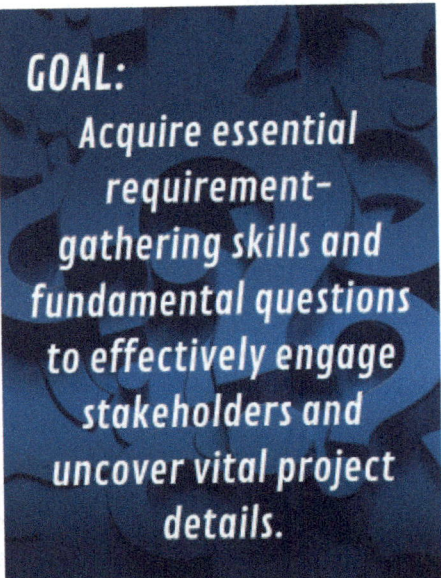

GOAL: Acquire essential requirement-gathering skills and fundamental questions to effectively engage stakeholders and uncover vital project details.

10.2.1. Project Goals

Here are a few questions that you may want to consider asking your key stakeholders to help you better understand the goals of the project and any underlying motives of the business for making the requested changes.

- ✦ What problem are we trying to solve?
- ✦ What are the goals and objectives of this project?
- ✦ What issue is the business facing and why is that a problem?
- ✦ What would happen to the business if we do not solve this problem?
- ✦ Who is experiencing the problem?
- ✦ Who's affected by the problem?
- ✦ Is there a workaround in place?

Asking these simple questions will help your understanding of what changes will be required for the system and the level of impact the changes will have on the business

Stakeholders

Now that you've begun to understand what problem the business is trying to solve, it's time to ensure you have included all the key stakeholders who should be involved in your project

> A stakeholder is someone who is interested in the outcome of your project. They are a member of the project team, but they do not contribute to the work being done.

We're about to review some questions that can help lead you to a list of all your stakeholders for your project. But before we do, let's look at project stakeholders in general and make sure we understand who a project stakeholder is.

A stakeholder is someone who is interested in the outcome of your project. They are a member of the project team but they do not contribute to the work being done. Stakeholders can even be people outside of your organization who would benefit from or be impacted by the success or failure of your project.

In other words, a stakeholder is basically someone who's got a vested interest in getting done whatever it is that you're trying to get done.

They are a part of the project team but they don't contribute to the work being done; meaning that one of your Salesforce developers or someone else who's actually contributing to work being done is not going to be considered a stakeholder.

What are the primary roles of the stakeholders on a project team?

✦ Stakeholders might be there to supply project requirements.

✦ Stakeholders may be involved to perform quality assurance testing or user acceptance testing.

✦ Stakeholders could be there for executive support. Meaning it's someone who holds a position with some level of authority or has the ability to get things done within your company, and their involvement as a stakeholder is to ensure that you get the resources that you need throughout the company, from all layers of management, in order to be successful in the project.

✦ A stakeholder could be a subject-matter-expert or business-process-expert. Sometimes those subject matter experts could even be from outside of your organization; for example, they could be a hired consultant or even from another company that is in a partnership with your employer.

There Are Three Types of Stakeholders:

01   Those involved in the day-to-day operations

02   Those impacted by day-to-day operations

03   Those supporting daily operations

It might be easiest to think of this not in terms of an enormous project but just as a specific change being made within your Salesforce Org.

To better understand this, let's consider an example of who would fall into each of these three types of stakeholders in an example scenario.

Who would your stakeholders be in this example scenario?

Example Stakeholder Scenario:
You are doing a project to improve the user interfaces on a sales opportunity in order to collect additional details at the time of a sales engagement.

Let's consider each type below:

01 **Those involved in the day-to-day operations:**
Those involved with the day-to-day sales and opportunity management are going to be your sales reps. It is the sales reps who would be completing any required fields on the Page Layout of the Opportunity record.

02 **Those impacted by day-to-day operations:**
Although a customer service representative would not necessarily be involved in those day-to-day sales activities, they are going to be impacted by it, because the activity that happens at the time of the sales engagement and the information that's collected there may later impact the ability for the service organization to best serve that customer.

03 **Those supporting the daily operations:**
And then you have the category of different operations teams, management teams, or others who are supporting the daily operations of the overall business in some way. Those individuals may not be directly involved in selling to the customer or servicing the customer, but there could be a variety of behind-the-scenes operational functions performed by these individuals in order for products and services to be delivered. These individuals may have metrics/KPIs that they're keeping track of, and they may be consistently required to report on those key performance indicators to senior business leadership. These individuals may wish to be involved in your project to give you input on additional data points that they would like for the sales reps to be gathering at the time of the sales engagement.

Hopefully this example helps you begin to understand the types of stakeholders who may want or need to be involved in a project, but how do you ensure that you have included all the key stakeholders who need to be involved for a successful project outcome?

Using Discernment When Identifying Key Stakeholders

You must exercise some level of discernment when identifying your stakeholders. If you exclude someone, then it may result in missing key details for your project and ultimately delivering a solution that is not the best for the business.

On the other hand, if you include too many people it may majorly slow down your project or even hamper any progress at all. Remember to "Fail Fast and Move Forward"; you can't do that if your team is too big.

One Man Seems Right Until Another Man Speaks

Back in one of the previous chapters when we discussed "Salesforce Jedi Wisdom," if you recall, one of the tips listed within that chapter was what I call the Proverbs 18 rule. Proverbs 18:17 states: "...the first to speak seems right, until someone comes forward and cross-examines." While technically, Proverbs 18 was referring to a lawsuit, you can apply the same principle to your requirements gathering process. I have often paraphrased this verse by saying "one man seems right until a second man speaks." When learning about a problem it's best to get multiple perspectives. Sometimes even really smart people are still wrong or misinformed. It can be easy to trust the opinion of one person, or, worse, to feel obligated based on the person's position or authoritative demeanor, but when requirements gathering, it would be prudent to get more than one opinion.

If you leave a key stakeholder out of the conversation, then it will lead to delivering half-baked solutions and create the need for rework, but add too many people and you'll have no progress at all. So how do you keep your team lean and agile but still identify and include all the key stakeholders that are needed? This can be bit of an art and a science, and some level of discernment is required.

Below are some questions that can help guide you in creating a list of all your stakeholders.

- **Who is involved in this project?**
  This is a nice open-ended question that can lead in any number of directions. By keeping things open-ended in your initial questions, it can uncover details that may be missed had you started off with assumptions or leading in a narrower way.

- **Who requested the change to the system?**
  As we previously mentioned: A stakeholder is anyone who's interested in the outcome of a project. If someone is asking for a change to happen within the system, then they would most likely have some interest in the "outcome" of getting that change accomplished. There's a pretty good chance that whoever initially requested the change to the system is going to be one of your stakeholders, or at least report to one of the stakeholders. For example, an individual Sales Rep may initiate a request for some changes to happen within your Salesforce Org, but it may be their manager who ultimately represents the sales team as a key stakeholder.

✦ **Who's experiencing the problem?** & **Who's affected by the problem?**
By who's experiencing the problem, we mean who is directly experiencing the problem; and when we ask who's affected by it, we are referring to the downstream impacts that may occur because of the problem. Let's go back to the previous example of someone in a sales role experiencing the problem of not having enough fields to store key customer information. Although the sale reps are the ones experiencing the problem, this same issue could have some downstream impact with negative implications on the service organization or on other stakeholders that are running reports/analytics.
While both of these are great questions to ask, it's important to ensure that whomever you are asking has the context of what you mean by each question. People by nature seem to be very good at focusing on the task at hand and figuring out how to do it better; but they are not always good at considering the larger picture and trying to understand how the task they are performing will have impacts on someone else down the line.

Some additional questions you may consider asking include:

✦ Who will be impacted by the project outcome?

✦ Who will be involved in the project decision-making process?

✦ Who will be providing resources (financial, personnel, equipment) for the project?

✦ Who will be responsible for managing and coordinating the project?

✦ Who will be the end-users of the project deliverables?

✦ Who will be impacted by any project delays or changes?

✦ Who will be responsible for testing and quality assurance of the project deliverables?

✦ Who will be responsible for the project's compliance with regulations and laws?

✦ Who will be responsible for the project's communication and progress updates?

✦ Who will be responsible for the project's risk management?

- ✦ Who will be responsible for the project's sustainability and maintenance?

- ✦ Who will be the main point of contact for the project stakeholders?

Most likely, the answers to these questions are going to lead you to most, if not all, of your stakeholders.

Additional Stakeholder Considerations

Your stakeholders should be people who are close enough to the problem to provide additional input to the development team as needed. And some of your stakeholders should be close enough to the problem to also be able to recognize viable solutions whenever you, your development, or architecture team create and proposes different design ideas for a potential solution.

Ideally, you would have someone within the group of stakeholders who know enough about the problem to immediately recognize that, yes, this can solve the problem or no, there's still going to be a gap.

This is why your stakeholders will be included in requirements gathering and design discussions. Their detailed understanding of the business processes related to the change will help you quickly confirm the probability of any suggested solution working and also help you quickly see whenever a suggested solution is not going to work. So, it's very important to have the right stakeholders on the team in order to prevent any rework from having to occur or prevent wasted time in going down a path that isn't going to work anyway.

10.2.2.   Key Deliverables

Key deliverables are the items that need to be completed and delivered in order for a project to be successful. If you consider all the things that must happen within your project in order for it to be considered completely finished, this can sometimes become a sizeable list. These deliverables can include things like user documentation, source code, testing procedures, technical diagrams, and deployment plans. The key deliverables may also specifically list out the desired functionality or features that are required to solve a problem faced by the business.

One method for gathering your key deliverables is to simply go down the list of your key stakeholders and ask each of them this one question:

> What would you need to have at the end of this project that you don't already have today in order for you to be happy with the project outcome?

It's worth noting that Salesforce.com is typically delivered in an incredibly agile way. If you're doing an enhancement to an existing Salesforce.com environment, then you're going to have much fewer deliverables identified as opposed to doing a brand new Salesforce.com implementation. Which is going to be a much larger project and therefore have more things to be delivered.

Generally speaking, the more specific we can be about what problem we're trying to solve, the better off we are, because then we can also be more specific about the objective evidence required in order to show that the problem is solved; and that becomes your key deliverables.

Problem Reduction

Problem reduction is a strategy used to reduce the complexity of a problem and make it easier to solve. This strategy involves breaking the problem into smaller, more manageable pieces and solving each piece individually. By looking at the individual pieces and understanding their relationships, one can see how they fit together to form a larger solution. Problem reduction can help make complex tasks simpler by allowing for creative approaches that take advantage of existing knowledge or techniques.

Problem Reduction can be helpful in taking a large amount of work and breaking it down into multiple work items, each with their own key deliverables, vs. trying to do too much in a single work item.

We do this by taking a big problem and breaking it into a collection of smaller problems, and then taking each problem in those collection of problems and continue to break it down even further and further, until eventually you get a problem that is small enough that it's something that you can just do.

If we look at how this relates to the scrum process and the work items that you'll have, you could have many different problems that you're trying to solve within a single project. Those problems are going to be represented as different work items that would be assigned within different sprints. Each of those work items would have their own key deliverables. So it's important to understand that if you were talking about doing an enormous project for a company, that enormous project could actually be broken down into a series of smaller projects. And then each of those smaller projects can be broken down even further into different work items. And each of those work items would have their own unique key deliverables.

Problem Reduction

| Take a big problem. | Break it into smaller problems. | Break each of these problems into smaller problems. | Eventually you get a problem so small that it's something you can just do. |

As you're asking the question 'what would you need to have at the end of this project that you don't already have today in order for you to be happy with the project outcome?' You're going to get very different answers depending on who you're talking to within the organization. Generally speaking, those higher in the organization may communicate at more of an epic level. On the other hand, the lower you go within the organization, they tend to communicate on more of a work item level.

The main point is, if you go down the list of all of your key stakeholders and you ask them for what the key deliverables would be for each of them, just expect widely varying answers and be prepared to segment that work as needed. By breaking the work into manageable chunks and getting the appropriate key deliverables for each chunk, it will help set you up for success. Remember that agile workflow is all about incremental improvement in order to get you to where you want to be.

10.2.3. Success Metrics

Success metrics are measurements used to evaluate the success of a project or goal. They can include quantitative performance data such as cost, time, and quality; or qualitative indicators such as customer satisfaction, employee morale, and team collaboration. Success metrics provide an objective way to measure progress and identify areas for improvement.

- ✦ Did you complete the project in the expected timeframe?

- ✦ Was there a specific budget set for the project? And if so, was the project completed within the set budget?

- ✦ Are all of the key stakeholders happy?

- ✦ Do you have any key stakeholders that feel like something was missed?

- ✦ Did you follow all of the Salesforce.com best practices for your deployments and everything that was built?

These are just a few basic but very meaningful things to look at to measure success. If all your key stakeholders are happy, you've met the needs of the business, you delivered within the timeframe that you were targeting, and you did it at or under budget… then that's a pretty successful project!

10.2.4. Deadlines

Project deadlines are dates set by a project manager to ensure the completion of tasks within a given timeframe. Deadlines can be used to organize, prioritize, and motivate people to complete their tasks on time and to the best of their ability. They also help teams stay focused and on track by providing a clear goal to work toward.

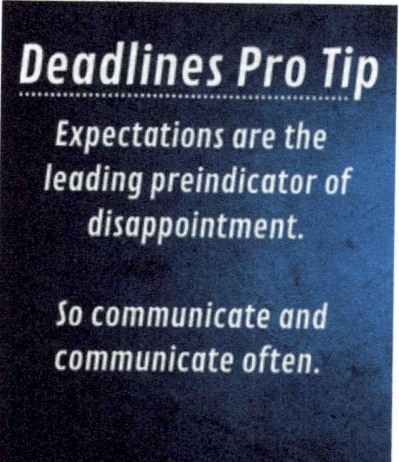

Deadlines Pro Tip

Expectations are the leading preindicator of disappointment.

So communicate and communicate often.

Setting Deadlines can be fairly straightforward, especially if you have a business that's demanding changes to be implemented by a certain date. But with that said, below are a few questions that you can ask yourself and things to consider before making deadline commitments.

Desired Timeline

What is the deadline that the business is desiring or has the business stated the desired timeline?

Bandwidth

Another thing to consider is your available bandwidth, as well as the bandwidth of the development team and any others who may be involved with the project. Do you have any other projects or competing priorities that may cause delays in this project's requested timeline?

Dependencies

Deployment dependencies refer to the relationship between different work items, where one work item depends on the completion of another work item before it can be deployed. For example, imagine that you are working on a software development project and one of the requirements is to implement a new feature that depends on the completion of a different feature that is currently being developed by another team. In this case, the new feature is dependent on the completion of the other feature and cannot be deployed until the other feature is completed and deployed.

Deployment dependencies can also refer to external dependencies, such as a requirement that a certain software version must be installed on users' computers before a new software release can be deployed.

In project management, it is important to identify and manage deployment dependencies to ensure that work can be completed in the correct order and to avoid delays. This can be done by creating a dependency matrix that shows which work items are dependent on which other work items and ensuring that the dependent work items are completed and deployed before the work that depends on them is deployed.

In addition, it's important to take into account the dependencies when setting deadlines to make sure that the project is delivered on time. If there are dependencies that will cause delays, it's important to communicate this to stakeholders and management as soon as possible so they can make adjustments to the project plan.

More tips for setting and managing deadlines:

- ✦ Understand the desired timeline set by the business or client.
- ✦ Assess the availability of the development team and any other stakeholders involved in the project.
- ✦ Identify and manage deployment dependencies between work items.
- ✦ Set realistic deadlines that take into account the complexity of the tasks and the availability of resources.

- ✦ Be prepared for changes and unexpected setbacks that may delay or prevent the completion of a project.

- ✦ Don't blame other people if you're not meeting your own deadline, just take responsibility for it and make adjustments.

- ✦ Communicate and communicate often. Communicate with your team members about any issues that arise during the project so they know what's happening. Communicate with all the project's stakeholders, and communicate up within the organization whenever necessary.

- ✦ Don't forget to include change management and software validation steps in your timeline. Even if you can technically complete all the Salesforce.com changes in a very short timeframe, there may be some extra work required to validate the changes and educate users prior to deploying the changes. If so, then the steps will need to be factored into the timeline.

- ✦ Use project management tools to track progress and ensure that deadlines are met.

- ✦ Prioritize tasks and set deadlines that align with the project's overall goals.

- ✦ Encourage accountability by assigning specific deadlines for individual tasks.

- ✦ Regularly review and adjust the project plan as needed to ensure that deadlines are met.

In conclusion, setting project deadlines is an important aspect of project management that helps to ensure that tasks are completed on time and to the best of their ability. By understanding the desired timeline set by the business, assessing the availability of resources, identifying and managing deployment dependencies, setting realistic deadlines, being prepared for changes, communicating clearly with stakeholders and team members, and using project management tools, project managers can effectively set and manage project deadlines to ensure the success of the project. It's important to remember that deadlines should be aligned with the project's overall goals and should be flexible enough to adapt to unexpected changes. By following these tips and best practices, project managers can ensure that their projects are delivered on time and to the satisfaction of all stakeholders.

SCAN ME

Explore Project
Management
Software Solutions

https://www.datasciencecompany.com/category/b
usiness-software/project-management/

How to Gather Project Requirements

10.2.5. Setting Priorities

Setting priorities is an essential aspect of project management. It helps to ensure that the most important tasks are completed first and that resources are allocated efficiently. Prioritizing tasks allows project managers to make the best use of their time, energy, and resources and to achieve the project's objectives. Prioritizing tasks also enables project managers to identify and mitigate potential risks and to make informed decisions about the direction of the project. By setting clear priorities, project managers can ensure that their projects are completed on time and to the satisfaction of all stakeholders. In this section, we will explore various strategies and techniques for setting priorities and how they can be applied to project management.

Here are just a few questions that that you can ask your project stakeholders in order to help ensure that you have the correct understanding of the priority level.

- ✦ What are the most critical aspects of the project?

- ✦ Are there any specific goals or objectives that must be achieved within a certain timeframe?

- ✦ Are there any external factors or dependencies that are impacting the project's priority level?

- ✦ What are the potential risks and consequences of not completing certain tasks on time?

- ✦ Are there any specific resources or constraints that need to be taken into consideration when prioritizing tasks?

- ✦ Are there any stakeholders who have a particular interest or concern about certain aspects of the project?

- ✦ Are there any legal, regulatory, or compliance requirements that need to be met?

- ✦ Are there any competing priorities or trade-offs that need to be made?

- ✦ Are there any specific metrics or benchmarks that need to be met in order to consider the project a success?

- Are there any areas where the project's priority level may change in the future?

- What is the priority level for the requested change?

- Do the Salesforce.com development resources need to begin work on it immediately? And if so, why? If not, what priority would be assigned to this work item?

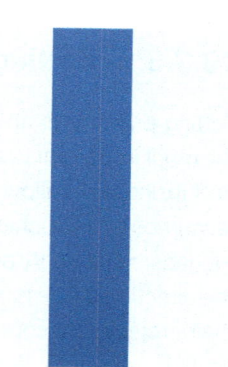

Managing Needy Stakeholders

In addition to the basic questions listed above, if you have a single project stakeholder who has numerous requests, then it can sometimes be helpful to get this stakeholder to weigh the different projects against one another to rack and stack them in order of greatest importance.

You can say something to the effect of:

> I understand this is very important to you and important to the business. Thank you so much for informing me of these details. Could you help me understand if we have to prioritize between this work item and this other work item? Which one do you believe would be the most important to you and the business?

This allows you to let them set the priority level and be in control while also making them aware that they may not get both items delivered at the same time. Let them be the one to tell you which one to work on first. And if you can accommodate that, that's great. Occasionally there will be technical dependencies or other limitations that mean you won't be able to deliver it within the desired timeframe. When this happens you will have to go back and educate them in accordance with the given situation. It's still very insightful to just have a dialogue.

Keep in mind that the purpose of all of the questions listed in this section help facilitate a dialogue. It's not necessarily as simple as a fill in the blank exercise, but it's more to get people's minds working so that they can really understand that there are only so many hours in the day and there's only so much that we can do as a Salesforce professional, project manager, or project teams; A very real world bandwidth limitation does exist, and sometimes this means that the business will be faced with difficult decisions on which work item they would like delivered first.

In conclusion, setting priorities is a crucial aspect of project management that enables project managers to make the best use of their time, energy, and resources. By understanding the most critical aspects of the project, identifying any specific goals or objectives, managing external factors and dependencies, identifying potential risks, and taking into consideration the specific resources and constraints, project managers can effectively set priorities. Furthermore, communicating and collaborating with stakeholders, taking into account legal, regulatory, or compliance requirements, being aware of competing priorities and trade-offs, and having clear metrics and benchmarks can also help project managers to identify and make the best decisions on setting priorities. By following these strategies and techniques, project managers can ensure that their projects are completed on time and to the satisfaction of all stakeholders.

Free Templates to Help Get You Started

REQUIREMENTS GATHERING TEMPLATES
FREE DOWNLOADABLE WORKSHEETS

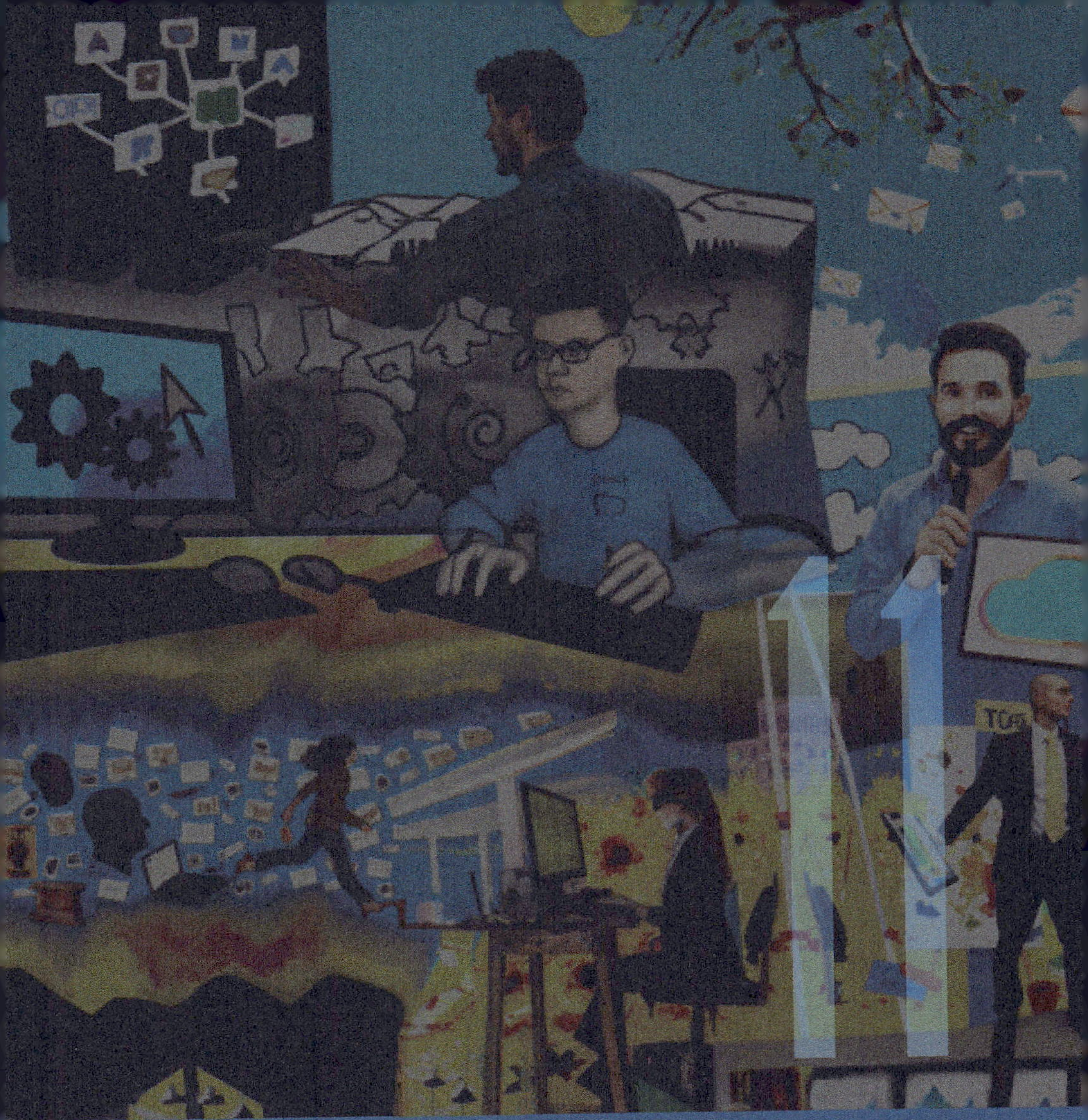

11

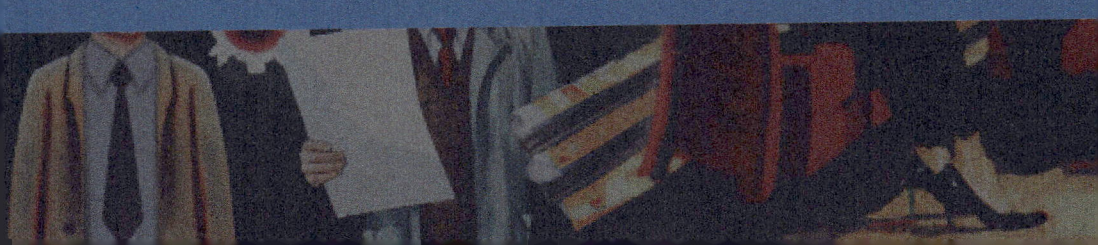

Understanding Different Salesforce Related Roles

11.1. Who Does What Introduction

We already discussed the different steps involved in the Software Development Lifecycle, and in this chapter we will discuss some of the different types of Salesforce roles to get a better understanding of who is involved with each step of the software development process.

We are not going to deep dive into all these roles, but it may be helpful for you to have some level of familiarity on the following eleven different job roles since each of these roles can be directly related to the Salesforce development lifecycle, and it's possible that as a Salesforce Administrator you will be engaging with others who work within these roles.

1. Salesforce Administrators

2. Salesforce Developers

3. Salesforce Consultants

4. Salesforce Architects

5. Salesforce Marketer

6. Salesforce Designer

7. Salesforce Business Analyst

8. Project Managers

9. Technical Writers

10. Scrum Masters

11. Quality and Regulatory (Q&R) or compliance representatives

Depending on the industry that you work in and the size of your employer, you may or may not directly encounter all of these roles within your day-to-day life as a Salesforce Administrator.

VHICH SALESFORCE CAREER
ATH IS RIGHT FOR YOU?

"WHETHER YOU CLICK OR CODE THERE IS A PATH FOR YOU"

SCAN ME

Learn More About Salesforce Career Paths

https://trailhead.salesforce.com/career-path/

11.2. Salesforce Career Paths

It's also worth noting that seven of these roles currently have a Salesforce.com certification path available.

Administrator
- *No Coding Required*
- *Build and Maintain*

Developer
- *Coding Expected*
- *Focus On Innovation; Not Maintance*
- *Cost More than Admin & Larger Skill Set*

11.3. Salesforce Admin vs. Salesforce Developer Comparison

We're going to begin with a quick high-level comparison of a Salesforce Administrator versus Salesforce Developer versus Salesforce Consultant.

Some people have had a lot of questions on these three roles, and there can sometimes be somewhat of a gray-area on when someone stops being an administrator and starts being a developer, but in short, there are two major differences in a Salesforce Administrator versus a Salesforce Developer.

1. **Code**

   Developers are expected to be able to code and administrators are not expected to code.

2. **Maintenance**

   Developers tend to build cool stuff and then pass it off to an admin to maintain. Administrators also have the ability to build cool stuff, but they typically get to also maintain it. The primary explanation for this is simply that developers tend to cost a company more than the administrator and they tend to have a more highly specialized skill set. So, it makes sense that most companies want their developers focused on building more cool stuff and solving complex problems for the organization and not resetting a user's password or performing other ongoing maintenance activities.

I've created the following infographics to help illustrate a few examples of the typical separation of duties from an administrator vs. developer. This is definitely an oversimplification, but I mainly want to focus on the differences between being an administrator and developer and also talk about how this relates to being a consultant. Let's start off by looking at the administrator and developer.

11.3.1. Manage Structure

At a high level, when it comes to managing the structure or data model of the Salesforce. com instance, both the administrator and developer have the technical ability to create apps and manage the data relationships.

MANAGE STRUCTURE			
Scope of Role	Salesforce Administrator	Salesforce Developer	Salesforce Consultant
Create Apps	✓	✓	✓
Create/Manage Data Relationships (Lookup or Master Detail)	✓	✓	✓

11.3.2.   Manage Visibility – Who Sees What?

When managing the visibility to "Who Sees What," both the administrator and developer can create and manage Sharing Rules. In addition, they can both manage the Role Hierarchy and the creation of Public Groups.

MANAGE VISIBILITY - WHO SEES WHAT?			
Scope of Role	Salesforce Administrator	Salesforce Developer	Salesforce Consultant
Sharing Rule Management • Criteria Based Sharing • Ownership Based Sharing • Manual Sharing	✓	✓	✓
Manage Role Hierarchy	✓	✓	✓
Manage Public Groups (Group Creation & Intended Use)	✓	✓	✓
Manage Public Groups (Ongoing Maintenance Add/Remove Users)	✓	☑☰☒☰☑☰	✓
Folder Management (Reports & Dashboards, and Communication Templates)	✓	☑☰☒☰☑☰	✓

Notice that we intentionally break out Manage Public Group's **Creation** vs. **Ongoing Maintenance.** It's true that both the administrator and developer have the technical ability to create and manage Public Groups. However, it is unlikely that the developer will spend their time doing the ongoing maintenance of the Public Group including adding and removing users as new employees are hired into the organization or terminated.

Likewise, while they both have the technical ability to perform Folder Management, these tasks commonly fall to an administrator versus a developer.

11.3.3.   Manage Permissions – Who Does What?

When managing the permissions on Who Does What within the Salesforce environment, it's likely that the administrator and developer will both manage profile settings. It's also likely that they'll both manage the Permissions-Sets and they could both manage the Org-Wide-Defaults.

PERMISSIONS - WHO DOES WHAT?			
Scope of Role	Salesforce Administrator	Salesforce Developer	Salesforce **Consultant**
Manage Profile Settings	✓	✓	✓
Manage Permissions Sets	✓	✓	✓
Manage Org Wide Defaults (OWD)	✓	✓	✓

11.3.4.   Manage Analytics – Reports & Dashboard Management

Both the administrator and the developer can manage reports and dashboards. However, this does tend to be more of an admin function.

ANALYTICS			
Scope of Role	Salesforce Administrator	Salesforce Developer	Salesforce Consultant
Report and Dashboard Management	✓	✓	✓

11.3.5. Organizational Management

For organizational management, both the admin and developer could manage any of the organizational features, including the Fiscal Year, the Business Hours, Holidays, Language Settings, Data Protection, and Privacy Settings.

ORGANIZATIONAL MANAGEMENT			
Scope of Role	Salesforce Administrator	Salesforce Developer	Salesforce Consultant
Fiscal Year	✓	✓	✓
Business Hours	✓	✓	✓
Holidays	✓	✓	✓
Language Settings	✓	✓	✓
Data Protection and Privacy	✓	✓	✓

11.3.6. Process Automation

Within the Process Automation category we start to see that there are some big distinguishments between what it means to be an administrator versus developer.

While both the admins and developers could create manage Workflow Rules and Workflow Actions, Create and Manage Flows, and they can both Create and Manage Process Builder Processes; the administrator would not be expected to manage code, so therefore they would not be expected to create and manage anything APEX related, nor would they be expected to do any management of Visual Force Pages or creating Lightning Components.

On the other hand, it is expected that the developer would be able to code and perform all these activities.

Notice that while the administrator isn't expected to be able to create Lightning Components, they are expected to be able to manage them on the front end. So, when the developer builds that new cool stuff in the form of a Lightning Component, the administrator can easily drag and drop the component and do any needed configurations directly in the user interface.

PROCESS AUTOMATION

Scope of Role	Salesforce Administrator	Salesforce Developer	Salesforce Consultant
Create and Manage Workflow Rules/ Workflow Actions	✓	✓	✓
Create and Manage Flows	✓	✓	✓
Create and Manage Process Builder Processes	✓	✓	✓
Create and Manage Apex (Triggers and Classes)	✗	✓	✓
Create and Manage Visualforce	✗	✓	✓
Create Lightning Components	✗	✓	✓
Manage Lightning Components	✓	✓	✓

These are just a few examples of how maintenance and code are two major distinguishing factors from a Salesforce.com administrator versus a developer.

11.4.   Salesforce Consultants

Now that we have covered the Salesforce.com Administrator and Salesforce.com Developer, let's discuss what it means to be a Salesforce Consultant.

You may have noticed that within the info graphics shown in the previous section ("Salesforce. com Administrator vs. Salesforce.com Developer"), it's possible for a Salesforce Consultant to do essentially any function that would need to be performed within Salesforce.

This is still a little bit ambiguous, because there's a few different types of Salesforce Consultants, and not all of them would be able to perform every function. Here we find some industry specific language that may slightly vary from the generally accepted definition of a "consultant." At a high level, we can break these "consultants" into two different groups:

- **The traditional definition of a consultant** - Either an individual or consulting firm that provides professional advice or services to an organization. These consultants have specialized knowledge and experience in Salesforce.com implementations and are hired to advise companies on how to best adopt Salesforce.com within their business, or they are hired to run specific Salesforce related projects to develop custom functionality within the company's Salesforce environment. These consultants may provide broader opinions on strategy and operations, as well as identify problems within the company's workflow processes and develop plans for corrective action.

- **Salesforce Certified Consultants** - Individuals who have one or more Salesforce. com Consultant Certification. These individuals may be employed by a consulting firm, but they may also work as an employee directly for a company who utilizes Salesforce.com to enable their operations. These types of consultants may lack the ability to code and have a more specific focus on different parts of the Salesforce platform.

11.4.1.   Certified Salesforce Consultants

Salesforce offers multiple consulting certifications to help prepare individuals to become consultants and be fully qualified to consult businesses and organizations on how to adopt standard features within a particular area of Salesforce.com to maximize operational efficiencies within the business/organization.

For a very long time, there was only a couple of Salesforce Consulting Certifications. Today, Salesforce has branched out to now offer ten different consulting certifications as of January 2023. Each consulting certification focuses on a particular niche within Salesforce.

For example, a Certified Salesforce.com Sales Cloud Consultant would come in and consult an organization on how to set up their Sales Processes. This may include how to manage their Accounts, Opportunities, Leads, Sales Teams, Sales Territories, and so on.

As another example, a Service Cloud Consultant may come into an organization and consult on how to adopt the service features of Salesforce.com, such as Case and Work Order Management or Service Teams functionality.

The following descriptions of each of these ten consulting certifications, and the ability to schedule your certification exam, can be found at: https://trailhead.salesforce.com/en/credentials/consultantoverview

It's worth noting that basically all these consulting certifications can be acquired without knowing how to do any coding.

1. Education Cloud Consultant

Education Cloud Consultant

The Salesforce Education Cloud Consultant credential is designed for consultants who have experience implementing Salesforce Education Cloud solutions in a customer-facing role.

2. Experience Cloud Consultant

Experience Cloud Consultant

The Salesforce Experience Cloud Consultant credential is designed for those who have experience implementing and consulting on Experience Cloud in a customer-facing role. Candidates also should be able to troubleshoot and solve platform issues.

3. Field Service Consultant

Field Service Consultant

The Salesforce Field Service Consultant credential is designed for individuals who have proven experience with the administration and configuration of Salesforce and are capable of consulting with customers on field service operations.

4. Marketing Cloud Consultant

Marketing Cloud Consultant

The Salesforce Marketing Cloud Consultant credential is designed for those who can set up and implement the Salesforce Marketing Cloud email application tools, providing solutions to execute both tactical and strategic email campaigns. Candidates should possess broad knowledge of Salesforce applications, regularly configure and manage Salesforce, and work with stakeholders to define requirements.

5. Nonprofit Cloud Consultant

Nonprofit Cloud Consultant

The Salesforce Nonprofit Cloud Consultant credential is designed for consultants who have experience designing and implementing Salesforce Nonprofit Cloud solutions in a customer-facing role that meet business requirements.

6. OmniStudio Consultant

OmniStudio Consultant

The Salesforce OmniStudio Consultant credential is intended for individuals who have experience consulting on building cloud applications using OmniStudio tools in a customer-facing role.

7. Pardot Consultant

Pardot Consultant

The Salesforce Pardot Consultant credential is designed for those who have experience implementing Pardot solutions in a customer-facing role. Candidates should be able to design and implement Pardot solutions that meet customers' business requirements and contribute to their long-term success.

8. Sales Cloud Consultant

Sales Cloud Consultant

The Salesforce Sales Cloud Consultant credential is designed for those who have experience implementing Sales Cloud solutions in a customer-facing role. Candidates should be able to successfully design and implement Sales Cloud solutions that are maintainable and scalable, and contribute to long-term customer success.

9. Service Cloud Consultant

Service Cloud Consultant

The Salesforce Service Cloud Consultant credential is designed for those who have experience implementing Service Cloud solutions in a customer-facing role. Candidates should be able to successfully design and implement Service Cloud solutions that meet customer business requirements, are maintainable and scalable, and contribute to long-term customer success.

10. Tableau CRM & Einstein Discover Consultant

Tableau CRM & Einstein Discovery Consultant

The Salesforce Tableau CRM & Einstein Discovery Consultant credential is designed for consultants who have experience designing and implementing on the Tableau CRM & Einstein Analytics and Discovery platforms in a customer-facing role.

So when we talk about these Certified consultants, it's those who aren't necessarily coders but they specialize on certain platform level functions.

11.4.2. Consulting Companies/Consulting Firms

However, you could also have the more traditional consultants for hire that come in to assist a company with their Salesforce.com Org. These consulting companies frequently include coders who work as consultants within the Salesforce framework. These consultants will typically also be certified Salesforce.com consultants; however, they are not only capable of helping a company adopt the standard Salesforce.com features, but they're also capable of coding custom solutions when required.

So just remember that the title of "consultant" by itself doesn't necessarily make it clear what an individual's capabilities are; dive deeper and ask questions about the individual consultant in order to learn if they're a consultant in one of these particular Salesforce.com certified consulting channels or if there are a more generalized consultant with the knowledge in some of these areas, plus the knowledge of how to code and create custom solutions.

Could Consulting Companies Help Jumpstart Your Career?

There is a slew of companies that offer Salesforce.com consulting. Some of these consulting shops are big and some are small, but Salesforce.com consulting companies are very popular, and you may one day find yourself working as an administrator within one of them. I've personally received a large volume of recruiters reaching out to me on LinkedIn each month to see if I would be interested in various employment opportunities. I've also received a number of them reaching out to me desiring to offer their consulting services to my company.

The fact that we still see such high demand from recruiters suggests that this is a space in the market that is still rapidly growing.

If you're new to Salesforce, then a Salesforce Administrator Certification is the place to start, but if you are looking to expand your career, then a Consulting Certification may be worth your consideration.

Learn More
About Salesforce
Consulting

https://trailhead.salesforce.com/en/career-path/consultant

11.5. Salesforce Business Analyst

Business Analysts play a key role in assisting with Salesforce.com projects. The Trailhead career overview offers the following message to business analysts, which provides some insight into the role.

A MESSAGE TO BUSINESS ANALYST

> You thrive on data and providing key business insights based on analysing multiple data sources. You take initiative to identify what the business should be tracking and evaluating, and you are able to think through the problems and make actionable recommendations.

To elaborate on this from my personal perspective, it's important that a Salesforce.com business analyst:

+ Have a moderate understanding of Salesforce.com.

+ Understands the business they serve.

+ Have the ability to work with key stakeholders in the business to define business requirements and develop user stories.

+ Can create process flows using Visio or PowerPoint (or other resources) to help communicate both the current processes as well as the desired future processes to all stakeholders.

In summary, a Salesforce Business Analyst is going to help with a lot of requirements gathering, problem solving, and root cause analysis.

They're going to help the business understand what problems they need to focus on, and they're going to help the development team understand how to best address those problems.

Business Skills Required

The general business skills required to be a Salesforce.com business analyst include:

+ Communication Skills

+ Organization Skills,

+ Writing

+ Project Management

+ Problem Solving

+ and generally speaking, being Detail Oriented

Learn More About Salesforce Business Analyst

https://trailhead.salesforce.com/en/career-path/business-analyst

11.6.   Salesforce Marketer

The Salesforce Marketer role is responsible for creating targeted marketing campaigns to connect with customers and deliver a personalized and effective customer journey.

Salesforce offers comprehensive marketing solutions including:

Content Marketing

Content marketing is all about creating engaging stories that help build brand awareness and grow an online presence. Shareable content is key, and metrics can help track success.

Product Marketing

As a product marketer, you will need to research current trends and use this information to help position your company's products. You will also be responsible for creating messages that highlight the benefits of your products to customers across various channels.

Demand Generation

Generating demand means understanding your buyers and target audiences and then reaching out to them with personalized offers. Real-time data and account-based marketing help you target potential customers more effectively.

Email Marketing

Get more people to click on links in your campaigns, get inactive subscribers interested again, and add new subscribers with an email solution made for businesses.

Marketing Analytics

Marketing analytics is the process of exploring data to better understand customer behavior and how it impacts revenue. You can use marketing metrics to personalize the customer experience and make it more tailored to their needs.

Data Analytics

Data analytics can help you see your customers better. You can see what they do and what they like. This helps you work more efficiently and make better decisions about marketing, selling, and customer service.

Marketing Leader

As a marketing leader, it's important to stay up to date on the latest industry trends and innovations. This way, you can stay ahead of the competition. Additionally, find new ways to engage with your customers and lead your teams with empathy.

11.6.1.   Salesforce Marketing Certifications

Salesforce Marketing Cloud Certifications are designed for professionals looking to demonstrate their knowledge and skills in Salesforce marketing initiatives. The certifications cover a variety of topics, including email marketing, web personalization, social media engagement, customer segmentation, and analytics.

The following descriptions of each of these six marketing certifications, and the ability to schedule your certification exam, can be found at: https://trailhead.salesforce.com/en/credentials/marketingoverview

It's worth noting that basically all these consulting certifications can be acquired without knowing how to do any coding.

1. Marketing Cloud Administrator

Marketing Cloud Administrator

The Salesforce Marketing Cloud Administrator credential is designed for administrators who can configure Marketing Cloud products utilizing industry and product best practices. Candidates should be generally familiar with data structure in subscriber data management and can thoroughly navigate Setup. Certified Marketing Cloud Administrators can successfully troubleshoot account configuration and user requests.

2. Marketing Cloud Consultant

Marketing Cloud Consultant

The Salesforce Marketing Cloud Consultant credential is designed for those who can set up and implement the Salesforce Marketing Cloud email application tools, providing solutions to execute both tactical and strategic email campaigns. Candidates should possess broad knowledge of Salesforce applications, regularly configure and manage Salesforce, and work with stakeholders to define requirements.

3. Marketing Cloud Developer

Marketing Cloud Developer

Certified Marketing Cloud Developers have hands-on experience developing across the full platform. They create personalized, dynamic messages and landing pages, and are fluent in Marketing Cloud scripting languages. They're also experienced in advanced segmentation, reporting and analytics, and data configuration.

4. Marketing Cloud Email Specialist

Marketing Cloud Email Specialist

The Salesforce Marketing Cloud Email Specialist credential is designed for those who can demonstrate knowledge, skills, and experience in email marketing best practices. Includes message design, subscriber and data management, inbox delivery, and external integrations with the Marketing Cloud email application.

5. Pardot Consultant

Pardot Consultant

The Salesforce Pardot Consultant credential is designed for those who have experience implementing Pardot solutions in a customer-facing role. Candidates should be able to design and implement Pardot solutions that meet customers' business requirements and contribute to their long-term success.

6. Pardot Specialist

Pardot Specialist

The Salesforce Pardot Specialist credential is designed for those who can demonstrate skills and knowledge in designing, building, and implementing marketing workflows through the Pardot platform.

Learn More About Salesforce Marketers

https://trailhead.salesforce.com/en/career-path/marketer

SCAN ME

JOIN US!

Understanding Different Salesforce Related Roles

11.7. Salesforce Designer

The Salesforce Designer career path is an exciting one that enables individuals to push the boundaries of innovation with the power of Salesforce in order to create user experiences that put people first.

The following descriptions of each of the two designer certifications, and the ability to schedule your certification exam, can be found at: https://trailhead.salesforce.com/en/credentials/designeroverview

Learn More About Salesforce Designers

https://trailhead.salesforce.com/en/career-path/designer

1. User Experience Designer (also known as "UX Designer")

User Experience (UX) Designer

The Salesforce UX Designer credential is intended for individuals who are aspiring or experienced designers wanting to build and design human-centered experiences on the Salesforce Platform.

2. Strategy Designer

Strategy Designer

The Salesforce Strategy Designer credential is intended for individuals with expertise using design methods to create compelling experience strategies that drive business outcomes using the Salesforce Platform. Candidates' skills span business, innovation, design & delivery.

11.8.   Salesforce Career Review & Summary

A Salesforce career path offers a wide range of opportunities for individuals to explore different areas of expertise and push the limits of innovation with these powerful technologies. With the right qualifications, certification, and drive, you can make your mark as a Salesforce professional and excel in whichever area you choose. The possibilities are endless!

The purpose of this high-level overview is to simply make sure you are aware of some the different career possibilities. There is a variety of different types of Salesforce roles, and what is right for one person may not be for another. However, a Salesforce Administrator role can serve as a launch pad to ultimately catapult you into other related roles such as Salesforce development, consulting, architecture, design, marketing, and more...

I truly hope you have found this book helpful, and I look forward to hearing from you as you continue on your Salesforce journey.

ABOUT THE AUTHOR

D E R E K D A V I S

Derek Davis, a seasoned tech professional, has dedicated the last two decades to learning various technologies for advancing his career and helping others do the same. With over a decade of experience in Salesforce leadership roles, Derek Davis has personally impacted the careers of many individuals in a variety of industries. Drawing from his extensive experience as a hiring manager and career coach, Derek Davis has distilled the key insights and tactics needed to succeed in a Salesforce career, making them readily accessible to anyone seeking to make the pivot. With a deep understanding of the Salesforce ecosystem and a passion for empowering others, Derek Davis is poised to make an even greater impact through his new book, which offers practical advice on securing a Salesforce job and thriving in the role. Whether you're a seasoned professional or just starting out, Derek Davis unique perspective and expertise make him the perfect guide to help you launch or advance your Salesforce career.

Made in the USA
Coppell, TX
05 August 2023

19986510R00077